Digital Futures:

Making Homes Smarter

David Gann, James Barlow,
Tim Venables

Published for the Joseph Rowntree Foundation
by the Chartered Institute of Housing

The Chartered Institute of Housing
The Chartered Institute of Housing is the professional organisation for all people who work in housing. Its purpose is to take a strategic and leading role in encouraging and promoting the provision of good quality affordable housing for all. The Institute has more than 15,000 members working in local authorities, housing associations, the private sector and educational institutions.

Chartered Institute of Housing
Octavia House, Westwood Way
Coventry CV4 8JP
Telephone: 024 7685 1700

The Joseph Rowntree Foundation
The Joseph Rowntree Foundation has supported this project as part of its programme of research and innovative development projects, which it hopes will be of value to policy makers and practitioners. The facts presented and views expressed in this report, however, are those of the authors and not necessarily those of the Foundation.

Joseph Rowntree Foundation
The Homestead
40 Water End
York YO30 6WP
Telephone: 01904 629241

Digital futures – making homes smarter
Written by David Gann, James Barlow and Tim Venables

Prepared for the Joseph Rowntree Foundation
Published by the Chartered Institute of Housing
ISBN 1 900396 14 9

Graphic design by Jeremy Spencer
Cover illustration by Liz Pichon
Printed by Hobbs the Printers, Totton

The home is by far the most important institution in the lives of the British people. It is a centre of interest, not only in the immediate family life, but equally in the wider hustling world of trade and commerce, for its influence is far-reaching and all-embracing ... The powerful influence of a well-run home is of national importance ... Never before has there been such a demand for well-built, scientifically planned houses. A new consciousness of home-making has been born. Men and women are equally enthusiastic. Together they study houses, plans and schemes of decoration; together they devise ways and means of owning homes of their own; and their interest is fostered and encouraged by manufacturers and designers of home equipment and household utilities. For indeed a modern, well-equipped home is a worthwhile possession, whether it consists of three rooms or thirty. It gives a sense of security and comfort and intimacy essential to real family life. Contributions to home services come from world-wide sources. Each year - almost each month - science brings some new discovery to the home. Ether waves are utilised for the preservation of food; wireless waves are made to boil water for the household; invisible rays protect the home from unwelcome intruders; and many other such wonders are rapidly being included in everyday household services.

From *The Home of Today*, published by Daily Express Publications, London c.1935, p.7: cited in Forty, 1986, p.114

CONTENTS

List of tables and figures

Tables

Figures

About the Authors

David Gann holds the IMI/Royal Academy of Engineering Chair in Innovative Manufacturing, carrying out research in construction and other project based industries. He is Professor of Technology Policy at SPRU where he leads the Programme on Innovation in the Built Environment.

James Barlow is a Senior Fellow at SPRU. He is currently researching the potential for 'mass customisation' housebuilding, and barriers to technical and business process innovation in the UK housebuilding industry.

Tim Venables is a research officer at SPRU, he is researching innovation in housing both in the UK and overseas. At the same time he is conducting his doctoral research into the diffusion of Information and Communication Technologies into the structure of the home.

Foreword

Smart Homes – what are they?

Cars have central locking, electric windows, remote controlled mirrors, CD auto changers – and the rest! And factories, offices and shops are often highly automated, giving staff control over their environments, and making buildings more efficient. Automatic doors, blinds that close when the sun comes out, infra-red lighting controls – they are all becoming commonplace.

But you don't find that sort of thing in people's homes much … or do you?

We *do* have remote controls for our TVs, we *do* have smoke detectors and passive infra-red burglar alarms, we *do* have timers on our central heating. But all these devices are separate entities. Each affects only one activity or aspect of the home.

Smart Homes are about something much more exciting. They are about using the latest information and communications technology to link all the mechanical and digital devices available today – and so create a truly interactive house. They started by designers examining the way people live now, and then exploring how society might look in the future. This generated a number of new ideas that could improve people's lives and help them stay independent for longer. Then the team investigated how existing technology could be used to turn those ideas into reality.

So it's not science fiction, its quite matter of fact – just some relatively simple technologies brought together – inventively – to create something rather special.

To test the ideas in reality the project created two *Smart Homes* – a Joseph Rowntree Foundation bungalow in York and an Edinvar Housing Association flat in Edinburgh. Both are only prototypes, but they represent the start of a revolution – because *Smart Home* thinking can be applied to any type of building.

We're not just talking about mansions for the very rich, or sheltered houses – although this technology is a godsend to people with disabilities, of course –we're talking about tower blocks, terraced houses, stately homes, crofts and cottages as well as newly-built homes.

And it's not just new build. *Smart Home* retrofitting involves less effort then rewiring – so existing buildings can easily be converted. The system is flexible and the components are getting smaller and more affordable all the time. In reality the applications are limited only by the imagination of the person installing it.

So here is just as a taster are some of the things you can do, starting with the front door.

You walk up to your house. One contact with the tag reader, and the alarm switches off … the door unlocks … and the lights and fire go on. And when a visitors calls, you could have any kind of alarm, such as lights flashing, for those who like listening to loud music, or the hard of hearing – or a spoken message, for the partially sighted. Then thanks to a tiny camera in the doorbell, the TV is automatically switched on to display a picture of the caller for instant identification.

Everything is completely controllable. This can be done by something that most people are probably comfortable with – a normal TV remote control. But instead of just changing channels, this can be used to open the front door, turn on the hall lights, light the fire, close the window, and even switch on the hi-fi.

There are infrared sensors in every ceiling, so it doesn't matter which room you are in – you can make things happen anywhere in the house.

For example, special extensions can give you remote control over any household appliance that plugs into a normal mains socket. Or you can build motors into the furniture, and do some more radical things like having cupboards that glide down for easy access, solving the dilemma of whether to have workspace or storage space in the kitchen. Or you can have a sink that goes up and down – ideal for households where one person is in a wheelchair. Or where the children can actually be persuaded to do the washing up!

And of course you can have normal switches for all these features, as well as the remote control.

But the *Smart Home* is not just about push button control. It really comes into its own when your choices are enhanced by information from the various sensors that are built into the house. The system knows which doors and windows are open, which are closed, how warm each room is, what the weather's doing, if there's any smoke or gas in the atmosphere – it even knows which rooms have people in them thanks to the passive infrared detectors. It can also be programmed to do certain things at certain times of the day, like switch on the central heating – or changing the lighting, or checking for activity around the house.

So, say you like to listen to the radio in the evening while you are getting ready for bed. You can set up the system so that the radio will come on automatically when you step into the bedroom but only if it's after 10.30 pm. Or you can have it so that the radio wakes you up in the morning, the kettle comes on to boil as soon as you sit up, and the bath starts running as soon as your feet hit the floor.

And don't worry about it overflowing, there are checks and safety mechanisms built into everything. For example, the bath is timed to fill for exactly seven and a half minutes, and it can even add hot water to take account of the air temperature in the bathroom!

There are virtually no limits to this kind of thinking. Curtains which close when it gets dark are already available – but wouldn't it be handy if the windows also closed – to just a crack when it's chilly, or nice and wide on balmy summer nights? Or, again only in the summer, how about if the window stayed shut to keep insects out while you read your book, then opened automatically when you turned off the light!

Of course *Smart Homes* also offer some serious benefits when it comes to safety and security. The gas detectors will detect any gas leak, so the system can switch off the gas before an explosion can happen. Or the smoke detectors can be hooked up to a local monitoring system. You could use infra red to check that people are OK, maybe sending an alarm to a warden – or by phone to a relative – if there's been no movement by, say, 10.00 in the morning.

In creating *Smart Homes* the aim is not to automate for the sake of it, but to build up a specification that responds to real needs which people may have. The report identifies four groups who might benefit especially – households in which both partners are working, highly mobile households, families in middle age, and people with physical disabilities and older people. *Smart Homes* ideas can help people to make better use of their home, do more things there and (in many cases) live more independently.

Many people are convinced that *Smart Homes* will be commonplace within a very few years. This study looks at the potential and the possibilities, based on experience of the two trial homes. Much of it is concerned with the technicalities – but with the aim of bringing the concept of the *Smart Home* closer to reality, especially for those who are elderly or have disabilities, for whom the benefits are only too obvious. We hope that it will start a debate about the usefulness of *Smart Home* technology, and lead to much greater awareness of its possibilities.

Chartered Institute of Housing and
Joseph Rowntree Foundation
September 1999

Acknowledgements

We wish to thank the Joseph Rowntree Foundation and Scottish Homes for supporting the research for this report. We are particularly grateful to Edinvar Housing Association and Joseph Rowntree Housing Trust who provided demonstration sites in which *Smart Home* technologies were installed. The project would not have been possible without the enthusiasm and endeavours of Robin Burley and Steve Bonner at Edinvar, and Peter Giles and Colin Taylor at the Joseph Rowntree Housing Trust. At times, it seemed against all odds that Colin and Steve managed to make progress on the demonstration sites, dedicating many evenings and weekends to procuring, installing, integrating and commissioning systems. Without them, we would have had no means of showing and testing the technology. We wish to thank the many suppliers of equipment and systems who helped in numerous ways to produce the demonstration dwellings. We are grateful to the EIBG and BRE for hosting the suppliers' workshop. Clare Xanthos surveyed other European *Smart Homes* projects.

We are also grateful to members of the Advisory Group who provided valuable information and guidance throughout the research. Members of the Advisory Group included:

Julie Cowans – Joseph Rowntree Foundation
Jane Scott – Scottish Homes
Tracey Roose and Mary Hopkinson – Anchor Trust
Clare McKenna – Oxford Brookes University
Phil Buckle and Graeme Wool – Electrical Contractors' Association
Bob Harris – R T Harris & Son Ltd
Peter Colebrook – Strategic Engineering
John Gill – Royal National Institute for the Blind
Helen Forsyth – Edinvar Housing Association
Robin Burley – Edinvar (now an independent consultant)
Charlie Legg – Housing Corporation (now a consultant)
Peter Lloyd – Sussex Gerontology, University of Sussex

We wish to thank the many potential users and carers for sparing their time to provide us with views on specific requirements, participating in focus groups and interviews. We are particularly grateful to Peter Senker for his paper on the role of carers. A large number of people completed our questionnaires in the demonstration houses, we are grateful to them too.

We wish to thank Ken Bromley of the Building Research Establishment for his work in analysing the issues concerning Technical Standards. This is reproduced in Appendix 2.

Finally, we are most grateful to Ritsuko Ozaki for her comments on early drafts of the text and to Charlotte Huggett for her assistance throughout the project, and in preparing the final report for publication. Nevertheless, we remain solely responsible for any errors in the content.

David Gann, James Barlow and Tim Venables
SPRU, University of Sussex
April 1999

In 1998, the Edinvar Demonstration Home won three awards:

- National Housing Award organised by the Chartered Institute of Housing and *Inside Housing* magazine
- Award for Innovation in Social Housing in Scotland, sponsored by the Scottish Office
- 2000 Homes Innovation Award

A video, showing the demonstration houses in use, and CD-ROM providing design details have been produced to accompany this study.

SUMMARY

Smart Homes are about more than automating routine domestic tasks and providing safety, security and environmental control. New Information and Communication Technologies provide an infrastructure which can support a wide range of new activities in the home, ranging from shopping, banking and working, to learning, entertainment, healthcare support services.

Many people are rightly sceptical about introducing more technologies into their homes, others are fearful of the problems this may cause. This study provides a critical assessment of issues relating to design, specification and installation of *Smart Home* systems.

❑ Aims of the project

The study presents the findings of a research and implementation project carried out between October 1996 and March 1999. The aims were to:

- produce a model user specification for the development and use of *Smart Home* technologies in the affordable and social housing markets. The specification is presented at the end of chapter 4;
- assess likely markets for *Smart Home* technologies;
- evaluate supply-side issues and lessons from integration and installation in the two demonstration projects.

❑ Main findings

- *Smart Home* markets, technologies and supply industries are immature: consumers are ignorant or sceptical about potential benefits;

technologies are difficult to integrate for interoperability; the industry is fragmented and there are no one-stop-shop suppliers providing a full range of bundled products and services.

- There is little standardisation across industries and countries and the development of common protocols to facilitate interoperability has been slow.
- There are no cheap appliances readily available to work on affordable systems.
- The pace of technological change is rapid. Lifestyles and the demand for new functions within the home are changing equally fast. Once potential benefits of integrated *Smart Home* systems have been proven it is likely that more people will be prepared to purchase them – in a similar way to investment in electricity or central heating in the home earlier this century. Systems will then begin to diffuse throughout the housing stock, costs will fall and a new supply industry will emerge.

❑ Main recommendations

- Producers of new housing and those responsible for major refurbishment work should provide an infrastructure to enable connectivity to new Information and Communication Technologies inside and outside the home.

  This *generic infrastructure* should provide the facility to connect to *context-specific systems* designed and installed to meet the needs of a broad range of users in different types of dwellings, with the capability of supporting *personalised systems*, tailored to specific individual and household requirements.
- In some cases, cableways can be provided at little or no additional cost. However, the routing of these must be carefully planned by someone competent to design a system that will meet a wide range of potential user needs. Access to cableways should be provided to accommodate future changes in information and communication technologies.
- New skills are needed, particularly in understanding user requirements and in integrating and installing systems.
- Further research is needed to understand benefits and problems of using *Smart Home* systems and to explore issues concerning adaptation, maintenance and service provision.

❑ Potential markets and user needs

There are five main reasons for the slow growth in markets for *Smart Home* systems:

- poor understanding of user needs on the part of suppliers and designers;
- lack of information about potential benefits and fears about systems operation, failure, loss of privacy and other ethical issues on the part of users;
- difficulties in integrating and installing systems, including lack of common standards;
- the cost of equipment and systems – they are too expensive to be affordable in low-cost and social housing;
- immature technology, causing concern about systems defects, rapid obsolescence, and potential upgradability and adaptability.

Nevertheless, there is a large and growing potential market for *Smart Home* technologies. The market ranges from young people with interactive educational and entertainment requirements to the growing number of elderly people who have a wide range of health and care needs. In the coming years, many people are likely to carry out more routine functions from their homes, including shopping, banking and paying bills, and some aspects of their work.

Technical requirements therefore vary considerably depending upon the type of property and individual circumstances. Many people are also concerned about issues such as safety and energy use in the home and digital technologies can be of use in managing these safety and energy systems.

Smart Home technologies could be used by occupants, visitors, carers and service providers in the home in four functional areas relating to:

- general labour-saving technologies around the home;
- technologies designed to assist in management and adaptation of internal environments;
- interactive systems for communication between the home and the world outside;
- assistive devices and systems for older people and those with disabilities.

❑ Demonstration sites

Two demonstration sites have been established by Joseph Rowntree Housing Trust in York and Edinvar Housing Association in Edinburgh. Trial systems have been installed at these sites for assessment by users and others associated with housing management and the provision of services in the home. It was not possible to purchase off-the-shelf components that could easily be assembled in customisable, plug-and-play systems. Systems had to be integrated, and in many cases, components were modified to achieve satisfactory solutions.

❑ Costs

The cost of equipment installed in the demonstration projects was in the region of £1400 per room. This was far higher than the target of a few hundred pounds per room, to prove affordability. However, more equipment was installed than would be necessary in many ordinary applications. For this reason, and because of the one-off nature of the demonstration projects, insufficient evidence was available to evaluate likely future costs. Larger-scale demonstration projects could provide better data in future.

❑ Housing providers

The main lesson for private housing developers, social landlords and housing contractors wishing to install *Smart Home* systems is that they will need to invest in new skills. Both the housing associations in this project have invested heavily in systems integration and user-interface skills, without which it would have been difficult to develop the demonstration sites.

❑ Technology suppliers

A narrow technology-driven approach persists amongst many suppliers who have so far generally failed to take adequate account of user needs or of systems integration and installation issues. User interfaces tend to be cumbersome to operate and equipment is usually designed for particular standards which hinder the type of interoperability required for costs to fall and markets to grow. Moreover, systems are mainly based upon those developed for office buildings and they are often over-engineered and expensive when applied in housing.

In future, emphasis should be placed on *functionality* rather than *technical features* in order to sell *Smart Home* systems. People are more interested in what new technologies offer in terms of improvements to their daily lives rather than detailed technical specifications.

Suppliers need to develop better interfaces and improve interoperability between sub-systems and components.

New systems integration service providers are emerging. There is likely to be increasing demand for firms with this type of expertise if markets begin to expand.

❑ Government

In future, the use of *Smart Home* systems could provide a variety of benefits to users and housing providers including access to new interactive services such as telecare, or lifelong learning facilities. Some of the capital costs of providing such systems could be off-set against savings in areas such as routine care and health checks. This has implications for inter-departmental policies, for example between the Department of the Environment, Transport and the Regions and the Department of Health.

The provision of more functions in the home raises a number of issues about quality of life, how it is delivered and how it is measured. New indicators are likely to be needed to measure housing quality including issues such as provision of technical infrastructure and support, to provide access to new Information and Communication Technologies.

❑ Standards

Common standards are required to provide interoperability between sub-systems and components. When bespoke, proprietary standards are used they can lock users into a particular set of equipment. Attempts to develop standard specifications are painfully slow and generally result in cumbersome documents with little general agreement on the way forward.

In consequence, the use of *Smart Home* technologies has been limited to those who can afford to pay for expensive one-off solutions, often based on security and entertainment systems.

❑ The future

Both Edinvar and Joseph Rowntree Housing Trust are involved in further research and demonstration work. It is essential that larger-scale demonstration projects are undertaken and that technologies are tested for extended periods with users. Results from these and other projects should help to build a new body of knowledge and capability to design, install and use *Smart Home* technologies.

CHAPTER 1

INTRODUCTION

The idea of introducing more technology into our homes may fill many readers with horror – computers seem to go wrong for inexplicable reasons with alarming regularity. Others are surprised that we do not already live in wired-up, modern, clean, sustainable, affordable and healthy homes. For them, the notion of a fully automated house represents the ultimate technical utopia. Whatever our views, it seems that we cannot escape from an increasing reliance upon digital communication and control systems in our work, for our entertainment, leisure and travel, for dealing with illness and disabilities and for managing our homes. Our intention is to explore how technology can help people in their homes, rather than make their lives more complicated.

Over the last 15 years, Information and Communication Technologies (ICTs) have become ubiquitous. Computers control programmes in our washing machines and central heating, engine management systems and automatic braking devices operate in cars, digital signalling systems are used on our railways and funds are transferred automatically at supermarket checkouts. But whilst many of our household appliances and utilities are managed using small micro-processors we make little use of the potential to combine these technologies to alleviate routine and tedious tasks, or to facilitate greater independence for older people and those with disabilities.

This study focuses on the opportunities and constraints to harnessing benefits of ICTs in our homes. We use the term *Smart Homes* to describe homes in which ICTs have been installed to help control a variety of functions and to provide communications with the world outside (see: Moran 1993). Integrated systems controlled by microprocessors are at the heart of these new applications.[1]

There is nothing new about the *Smart Homes* idea, it became a popular term in the early 1980s around the time that the 'intelligent building' concept was first used in the USA.[2] But automation of domestic tasks has been the goal of many developments in mechanical and electrical products over the last 100 years or so. In the past 30 years an increasing range of electronic products has been developed, and added to existing appliances and systems in our homes. Consumer electronics, electrical equipment and heating and security systems manufacturers have been developing digital technologies for domestic appliances and consumer products. Service providers such as telecommunication companies, water, gas and electricity suppliers have been developing systems to provide new interactive services. Technologies and the services they provide continue to evolve at a rapid pace.

Yet there are no precise definitions of the technologies or functions involved. The new underpinning technologies involving computers, communication devices and network infrastructures – such as the Internet – have not yet reached maturity. Driven by the search for new mass consumer markets, hardware, software and service providers are developing new applications that they believe will offer people many new benefits in their homes.

Many people have not heard of *Smart Homes*. Moreover, a large proportion of those who are familiar with the term are unlikely to have a clear idea of what it means. For example, is it more than just another technological fad, dreamt up by marketing departments in consumer electronics firms, waiting for the right conditions to push technology into the marketplace?

The purpose of this study is to provide a critical appraisal of the direction, benefits and constraints to installing and using *Smart Home* technologies. Many of the technologies currently available are relatively expensive and are aimed at middle and upper income home owners. Our research and development work centred on testing these ideas in two demonstration projects, in the lower income and affordable housing markets, in consultation with different groups of users.

In the study we explain some of the underlying assumptions about specification, development, installation and use of new digital technologies in our homes. We evaluate the possibility of providing occupants with substantial improvements in the performance and use of their homes. We focus particularly on facilities that improve the quality of life at home and reduce costs in use. The areas covered include:

- safety
- security
- convenience and usability
- control of domestic appliances
- energy and environmental management
- new forms of entertainment
- business, homeworking and learning applications
- home services such as shopping, medical and care provision.

We set out to test whether it is possible to meet changing occupiers' needs and help them achieve greater independence, so that people can remain living in their existing homes for longer. Our contention is that appropriate *Smart Home* technologies could play an important part in advancing the concepts of flexibility and adaptability in *Lifetime* or *Barrier Free Homes*.[3] Such technologies could also increase the range of choices over how we live at home. Such benefits are only likely to be realised, if inexpensive, easy-to-install, simple-to-operate technologies are developed. Moreover, they will almost certainly need to be modular, expandable and upgradable operating on an open infrastructure, with simple user interfaces and communication protocols.

❑ 1.1 Questions about new technology in our homes

For much of the two and a half years we worked on this study we were confronted with more questions than answers. Some were of a purely technical nature, others related to economic, social, ethical and regulatory issues. For example:

- What are the consequences of *Smart Home* technologies for the ways in which we design, construct, adapt and maintain our homes in terms of physical structure and layout?
- How can we plan to get more from technology in our homes and what will it cost?
- How will systems and new services be paid for?
- To what extent do we need to integrate systems to achieve better value services and new functionality?

- How much do *Smart Home* technologies depend upon related infrastructure such as new cabling in our homes, or satellite dishes on our walls?
- Will we need to dig up our streets and garden paths, and disrupt the inside of our houses to make way for new cabling?
- How do these systems relate to, or depend upon other systems such as the telephone, transport, healthcare, banking, shopping, entertainment, water, gas and electricity, television, radio or the internet?
- What needs to be done to install a generic infrastructure that will facilitate the use of 'plug-and-play', or 'click and go' technologies which anyone can use?
- Who will supply the technology, how will it be installed, who will maintain and update it?
- Will *Smart Home* technologies be easy to operate and how might they affect what we do and how we live at home? Will people have adequate knowledge about their use?
- What types of systems would enable people with disabilities and frail older people to live more independently in their own homes?
- What problems might these technologies create for users, visitors, or professionals in housing, social services and healthcare?
- Are *Smart Home* technologies likely to be dangerous or stressful to use?
- Will people trust systems or fear that equipment may fail – are they fail-safe?
- Will there be adequate support and backup if systems do not function properly?
- Will *Smart Homes* provide people with more opportunity to socialise or will they create isolation?
- What are the ethical issues and social consequences associated with using ICTs in the home, including issues of remote surveillance and privacy?

In this study we provide answers and insights to these questions, drawing on the experience and lessons learned in developing two demonstration projects. We also comment on the rate and direction of technical change and discuss how digital technology might affect the ways we live at home.

❑ 1.2 About the research

It was with the questions in mind that we set out to develop and test two demonstration homes. Our previous studies on housing and home automation highlighted a number of reasons for failure in the technology-push approach.[4] We wanted to start with a better understanding of what people do in their homes and how technologies might be designed to assist them in everyday tasks. Moreover, we wanted to develop a specification for technologies in affordable and social housing markets. This project was the first of its kind to be driven by academic researchers pursuing a user-focused approach in affordable housing markets.

We began our work with a user needs analysis, running workshops to assess the potential for using new digital technologies in the home with different user groups in Edinburgh and York. These included people with a variety of physical and learning difficulties living in accommodation with on-site care services. Our workshops included people from different age groups, with a variety of needs and with different abilities in using ICTs. We also held workshops with carers and visitors to elicit their views about needs and potential uses of technology.

In parallel with our user needs analysis, we conducted a technical review of communications protocols aimed at assessing the potential for inter-operability of systems and their application in *Smart Homes* and residential buildings, including links to remote control centres. This review was carried out by Ken Bromley of the Building Research Establishment (BRE). It focused on applications such as the management and control of heating, ventilation and air conditioning (HVAC), lighting control, fire detection and prevention, security and access control (including the use of video), metering of fuel and power, telemedicine, etc.

A supplier workshop was held at the Building Research Establishment in collaboration with the European Intelligent Building Group (EIBG) with the aim of informing potential systems manufacturers and component suppliers about the specific needs of the project.

An outline specification was written for the two demonstration sites in York and Edinburgh, and tenders were invited from a short list of suppliers. The demonstration homes were developed by Joseph Rowntree Housing Trust in York and Edinvar Housing Association in Edinburgh. Components and systems were procured and installed in these homes for assessment by users and others associated with housing management and the provision of services in the home. An evaluation of supply-side, technical, installation, operation and maintenance issues was carried out. Users, carers and owners were invited to assess the systems and user reactions were analysed. The demonstration sites were opened to members of the public for several months, and visitors were asked to complete a questionnaire asking about their reactions to what they saw. This survey yielded 88 responses.

❑ 1.3 Structure of this study

This study is aimed at all those who have an interest in the future development of housing in the UK. The starting point was to understand the likely needs of users, occupants, residents and people visiting our homes, including carers, and people from health and social services. We hope that the study will be of interest to everyone from a user perspective. The report is also aimed at owners, public and private housing developers, housing finance organisations, regulators, technology suppliers, installers and the many different new digital service providers. For these organisations, *Smart Homes* may represent new market opportunities, or the need to find innovative solutions to construction, assembly, maintenance and adaptation. They may also require changes in regulations and building control.

The main body of this study is organised in five chapters. Chapter 2 provides the background to some of the key issues relating to the installation and use of technologies in our homes. There is an implicit assumption held by many people involved in our demonstration projects that the introduction of *Smart Home* technology has radical consequences for the ways in which we produce and use our homes. We explore this view with reference to previous periods of major change such as electrification in housing. Chapter 3 focuses on user needs and different markets for *Smart Home* technology, it provides the results from a number of focus-groups held with potential users and visitors to our homes. In chapter 4, we discuss trends in technology and requirements for interconnectivity and integration between systems. A functional specification for *Smart Home* systems is developed, drawing upon analysis of work with users and suppliers, and in consultation with Edinvar Housing Association and Joseph Rowntree Housing Trust. The experience of procuring, installing, operating and adapting *Smart Home* technologies in the demonstration projects in York and Edinburgh is discussed in chapter 5. This describes reactions from potential users of these homes and explains the results of our questionnaire survey of those visiting the demonstration sites. Chapter 6 concludes with a discussion of the main lessons for future projects, issues about how the market for home systems could expand, and recommendations for policymakers in various public and private sector institutions.

For readers wishing to review work of a more technical nature, we have included the technical specifications for both demonstration projects in Appendix 1. An assessment of different standards and communications protocols for *Smart Homes* is provided in Appendix 2, and a description of other European research and demonstration projects is given in Appendix 3. A list of useful Web addresses and resources is provided in Appendix 4. Some of the technical terms we have used are described in Appendix 5.

Notes

1 The term *Smart Homes* is used to describe homes in which ICTs have been installed to help control a variety of functions and to provide communications with the world outside. Others have called them 'computer homes' (Mason and Jennings 1983), 'electronic houses' (Mason 1983), 'intelligent homes' (Gann 1992b), 'interactive homes', 'home informatics' (Miles 1988), 'home telematics' and 'domotique', in France.

2 The 'intelligent building' concept originated as a marketing ploy by ShareTech, the ill-fated joint-venture between AT&T and United Technologies, established in the wake of the break up of the Bell telephone system. The concept spread quickly from the USA throughout Europe and Japan in the mid-1980s.

3 Others have approached this issue from the perspective of people's changing needs from their housing as they get older and their circumstances change. One specific perspective is the concept of flexibility and adaptability implied in *Lifetime* or *Barrier Free Homes* (Bright 1996; Burley 1994; McCafferty 1994; Martin 1993).

4 See Gann *et al* 1994 and 1995.

CHAPTER 2

THE EVOLUTION OF SMART HOMES

The *Smart Homes* concept is the latest expression of the various ways in which technology in the home has developed. This chapter looks at the history of home-based technology and how *Smart Homes* have emerged. It also considers how information exchange between the home and the outside world has developed, and the recent rapid growth in the use of the Internet.

❑ 2.1 Lessons from previous attempts to introduce technology in the home

The installation and use of technology in the domestic environment has played a major part in shaping the design and construction of housing over the last century. The introduction of new technology in the home can be understood at three levels. First, it has been necessary to connect houses to an external infrastructure, such as water and sanitation, gas and electricity supplies, telephone and increasingly, cabled television and other interactive services. Second, it has been necessary to provide a means of distributing basic utilities around the home on an internal network or infrastructure. Examples are plumbed hot and cold water, central heating and drainage for waste and soil; electrical wiring for power and lighting; twisted-pair cabling for telephone lines; co-axial cable for televisions. Third, there are the domestic appliances and terminal equipment themselves which connect to the internal infrastructure, providing a variety of functions and in some cases acting as interfaces between users in the home and the world outside. Technology is generally more portable and takes the form of consumer-goods at the appliance level, whilst in the first and second levels it is often embedded within the building, street or surrounding area, forming part of the fixed-capital infrastructure.

For the purposes of supporting everyday domestic activities, mechanical technologies have always been important and will very likely remain so for many centuries. The automation of routine physical tasks has successfully liberated us from drudge-work in the home and helped people with special needs to live more independently. They have been equally important in helping to reduce the risk of disease and illness. Issues concerning cleanliness and hygiene grew in importance in the late nineteenth century with better scientific knowledge about consequences for health. Widespread public understanding of these issues was closely linked with the successful development of new businesses for kitchen and sanitaryware product manufacturers: flushable water closets and manually operated washing machines, are among early examples.

The development of electric power represented a major technical change in our homes. Not only did it provide new, safer forms of light and heat, replacing gas and incandescent sources, it also provided a source of power for many hand-operated mechanical tools and aids in our homes. Moreover, from around 1915 onwards, electrification in the home brought with it the introduction of new electrically powered machines and gadgets for domestic use including vacuum cleaners (health and cleanliness), sewing machines (homeworking and repairs) and food-processors (home automation). A number of manufacturers grew to fame and fortune from the sales of electrical equipment, promising to ease the burdens of domestic work

Table 2.1: Examples of electrically powered equipment in the home

Kitchens	**General systems**
Kettles	Clocks and timers
Toasters	Boilers
Milk sterilisers	Radiators
Cookers	Thermostats
Potato peelers	Meters
Coffee pots	Water pumps
Egg boilers	Macerators
Food mixers and processors	Fans
Yoghurt makers	Alarms
Knife grinders	**Utility rooms and cleaning**
Dish washers	Washing machines
Bathrooms	Tumble dryers
Shavers	Sewing machines
Hairdryers	Vacuum cleaners
Toothbrushes	Irons
Entertainment	
Radios	
Music centres	
Televisions	
Telephones	

advertising everything from 'spring cleaning with electricity' to the 'all electric breakfast': examples of household brands include: Belling, Creda, Electrolux, Ferranti, Hoover and Kenwood. Table 2.1 illustrates a number of the more common electro-mechanical products that provide comfort, safety and remove routine chores in the home. The labour-saving house was a cliché of the 1920s onwards, with the introduction of the small electric motor. It was in part a response by the emerging middle-classes to the perceived shortage of domestic servants (Forty 1986: 118). The main aim was to replace domestic servants with machines, so that one person could look after the whole house with time to spare for other activities (Hardyment 1988: 177-179).

Most of us take electric light, power and associated appliances and consumer products for granted. But it was not so long ago that their introduction was accompanied by major upheaval both in physically locating them within our homes, and in terms of the ways in which we integrated these new functions in our daily lives.

The Electrical Development Association (EDA) played an important role in creating the conditions for the expansion of markets for these types of products. Diffusion into the market started in around 1900 and continued for about 30 years. Adrian Forty argues that in the mid 1920s, the conditions were right for demand for electrical appliances to grow. These included cheap supply of electricity, cheap and reliable appliances and the installation of a distribution and wiring system. There could be a number of parallels here with the potential growth of *Smart Home* systems.

Between 1918 and 1939, the extension of mains electricity supply to both new and existing houses meant that the proportion of households connected to the mains rose from 6% to about 66%. A large number of houses were equipped only for lighting between the inter-war years. Those houses that had electricity for power often only had one 5 amp socket. Probably only one third of all homes had more than two electric sockets, and they were principally newly built houses in the upper price bracket (Forty 1986: 189).

Moreover, people were fearful of the consequences of wiring up their homes. Anecdotal cases known to Adrian Forty include two old ladies who anxiously kept plugs in all the electrical sockets to prevent electricity from leaking out; another old lady was said to be terrified by the installation of even an electric bell lest the workman be killed in the process.

The need for labour-saving, hygienic, safe, and secure homes has been a priority for many decades. Manufacturers, installers and housebuilders have

Figure 2.1: Advertisements promoting the benefits of electricity in the home

Daily Mail, 1955

Electrical Development Association, 1928

US electric cooker, 1961

Hoover, 1927

successfully integrated many products into the home which have improved the standard of living and changed the expectations of occupants. These changes took time and were often closely related to changes in design and construction of new housing, particularly in bathrooms, kitchens, utility rooms and living rooms: the TV lounge. Houses were designed for new styles of living with modern technologies. This spawned new design services such as kitchen planning. A number of lessons can be taken from these experiences for the contemporary situation associated with the introduction of *Smart Home* technologies. Perhaps the most important are the conditions that need to be satisfied before markets are likely to grow. For example:

- a reliable infrastructure must be built and serviced;
- regulatory approval must be obtained after safety compliance testing for new equipment;
- safe, affordable and reliable appliances need to be produced and marketed;
- housing needs to be redesigned to accommodate new equipment and activities;
- cultural acceptance needs to be gained by demonstrating advantages and allaying fears.

In some instances, success has also been associated with free provision of technology to users. The contrast in growth of viewdata services in the UK (Prestel), with France (Minitel) shows that in the French case, the provision of free terminals was a significant factor in the successful adoption of the technology.

❑ 2.2 Home on the Net – a changing sense of place

Many of the products and systems listed in Table 2.1 now include microprocessor controls to enable users to select different performance functions. So called 'intelligence' has been added to domestic appliances. But given these experiences, is there something new happening with the introduction of ICTs to lead us to believe that the *Smart Home* concept will at last become a reality? There are at least two forms of *Smart Home* which are emerging because of different imperatives. One involves the traditional approach to home automation associated with the use of 'intelligent' domestic appliances. The other is more recent, involving interactive computing, communication and entertainment services within and beyond the home.

Major computer, software and entertainment services providers are beginning to explore the convergence of the more traditional automation aspects with newer informational features. Numerous writers and film-makers have speculated about future homes, sometimes in threatening, sometimes in comical terms. In many of these visions the home is seen as a physical access node for 'electronic spaces' within advanced communications networks. Typical is Alvin Toffler's notion of the 'electronic cottage' as a locus for employment, production, leisure and consumption (Toffler 1981). Common to many perspectives is a redefinition of the home to allow the household to reassume roles – such as work, education, medical care and entertainment – which have increasingly been externalised. Driving this is a desire by individuals to retreat from the environmental, social and political problems of late twentieth century industrial cities, with – according to Toffler – fundamental economic implications:

> *... if individuals came to own their electronic terminals and equipment, purchased perhaps on credit, they would become ... independent entrepreneurs rather than classical employees meaning ... increased ownership of the means of production by the worker. We might also see groups of home-workers organise themselves into small companies to contract their services or ... unite in cooperatives that jointly own the machines. All sorts of new relationships and organisational forms become possible.* (Toffler 1981: 223)

This utopian view of liberation through technology seems quaintly old fashioned now and as we argue below, the technologies upon which it was based have been developed, but the form of social use has generally not transpired.

The evolution towards the multi-functional home is also, some suggest, a result of changes in the spatial organisation of advanced society. As Lorente (1996) puts it, 'global houses' are needed if we are to live in 'global villages'. He argues that fully inter-connected housing can act as an interface between Castells' (1989) 'flow space' – the increasingly important network of information flows – and 'physical space', where the experience and daily life of most people takes place. In this way the home becomes the location from which people access information from anywhere in the world. Furthermore, the home will not only become a place for passive reception, but also an active producer of information and energy – the latter, for example, through the generation of solar electricity.

These perspectives which tend to be technologically determinist, or utopian, have been criticised because they reduce what are complex interactions to crude and homogeneous models of technologies and their urban impacts (Graham and Marvin 1996; Robins and Hepworth 1988). Furthermore, they tend to ignore the social and political processes through which technologies are actually developed and applied, especially the assumption that local social and political actors have little or no scope to shape developments.

More than 30 years ago Nicholas Johnson argued that:

> *The home will ultimately be the communication centre where a person works, learns, and is entertained, and contributes to society by way of communications techniques we have not yet imagined – incidentally solving commuter traffic jams and much of their air pollution problems in the process.* (Johnson 1967, quoted in Graham and Marvin 1996: 92)

During the 1970s and 1980s, in spite of the futuristic visions and hype of organisations with a vested interest in developing products and services, there was only limited progress towards the introduction of *Smart Home* technologies. To some extent the view expressed in 1989 holds true today, that:

> *... a combination of home computers, consumer electrical goods, videotext services, and home security systems, even in a "smart house", wired with heating and lighting sensors ... hardly adds up to a revolution in ways of living* (Forester 1989: 224).

In the 1980s and early 1990s manufacturers of integrated home systems had generally failed to develop mass-markets for their products and services. Technical standards failed to create the right conditions for the growth of mass-markets for *Smart Home* applications. Attempts to develop standard specifications have generally resulted in cumbersome documents (ESPRIT-HS Consortium 1991). One of the main problems was a narrow technology-push approach by suppliers who failed to take adequate account of user needs. Systems and components were expensive. User interfaces were cumbersome to operate and manufacturers' bespoke systems locked users into a particular set of equipment, failing to provide the type of inter-operability required for markets to grow. Markets failed to grow even in Japan, where there was huge investment in R&D and new product development: one of the reasons for market failure was the unacceptably complicated controls interface – see Figure 2.2. Between 1990 and 1995, home automation systems had only penetrated the market to a level of $\frac{1}{30}$ of that projected in the 1980s.

Figure 2.2: Japanese *Smart Home* technology which failed to achieve market acceptance

Bathroom controls

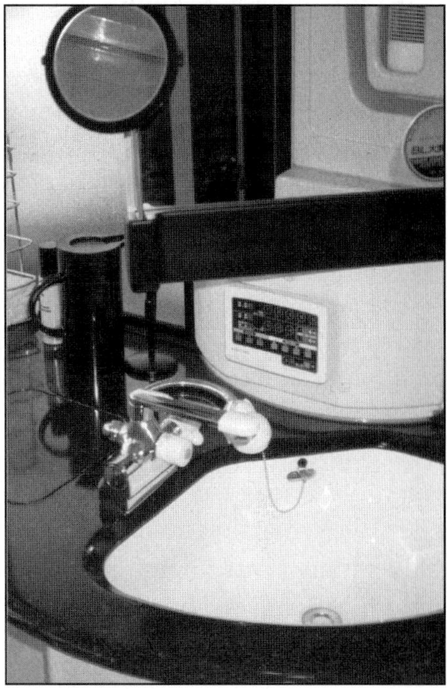

Bathroom controls

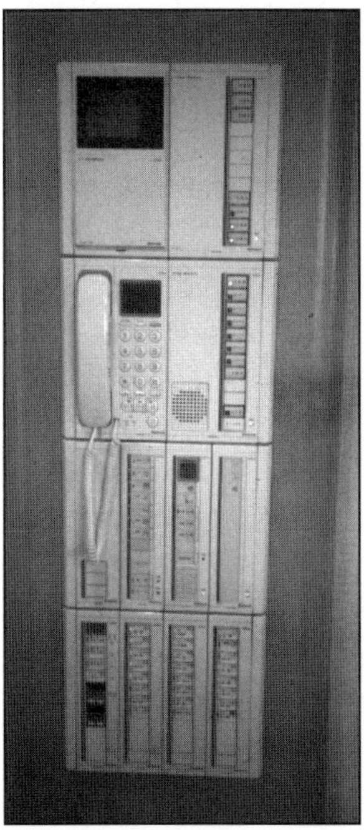

Central control panel

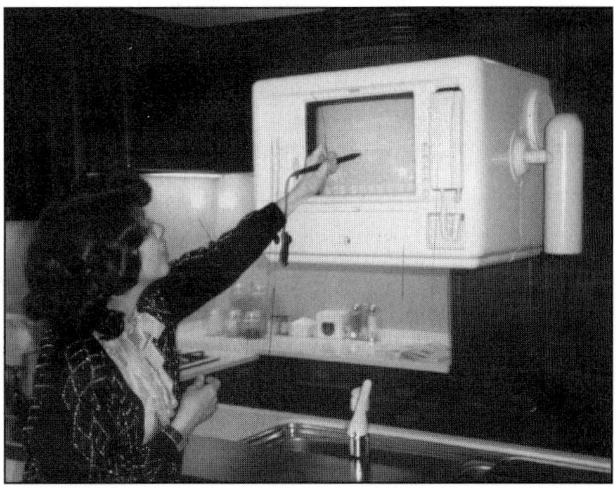

Kitchen robot

Attempts to develop standard specifications were painfully slow and generally resulted in cumbersome documents with little general agreement on the way forward. In consequence, the use of *Smart Home* technologies was limited to the rich and famous who could afford to pay for expensive one-off solutions, often based on security and entertainment systems. With the exception of some applications in the USA, there was a general trend towards acceptance of discrete technologies rather than attempts to provide fully integrated solutions. For example, markets for computer and video games, security systems and alarm call services all grew strongly, but there appeared to be little interest from purchasers or from most manufacturers to link systems together in a manner that would deliver the benefits described by the technological visionaries.

Nevertheless, significant changes have occurred in the use of information and communications technologies within our homes. Many systems that were once solely the domain of the office have now become 'domesticated' (Silverstone 1994). Digital ICTs are the most significant technology to be introduced into our homes since electricity, telephones, radio and television. Moreover, the pace of these changes has been extraordinary when compared with the speed of electrification or the rate of adoption of the telephone, TV or radio earlier this century.

For example, use of the Internet has been growing in Britain at a rapid rate in the past two years. An NOP Research Group study showed that nearly 11,000 new adult users are logging onto the Net every day. Some 11 million adults accessed the Internet at least once during 1998, a 48% increase compared with 1997. The location of Internet use has also changed with around 6 million people using the Internet from home by December 1998, compared with 3.4 million in December 1997 – a 76% increase. Around 1.3 million people shopped online in the second half of 1998 and the rate of expansion of Internet use is predicted to be 2% per month during 1999 (NOP Research Group – online information, and Financial Times coverage of report from E-Commerce, FT.com, January 1999).

In spite of its rapid growth in home use, access to the Internet continues to rely upon a cumbersome user interface, requiring keyboarding skills and perseverance on the part of the user to navigate through a confusing morass of information. Cawson and Lewis argue that the television appears to be a promising means for access to interactive services such as teleshopping and telebanking, but is not favoured for general Internet access. Apart from the telephone and television, Teletext is the most pervasive ICT in UK homes. In those households with access to the Internet, more time is being spent at the computer terminal, at the expense of time spent watching television (Jonscher 1999).

Whilst the main use of home PCs is for playing games, it is closely followed by use for educational purposes. Children usually have greater access to PCs at home than other age groups. This is consistent with views of parents who believe that ICTs can improve their children's education and that they make learning more enjoyable. But the importance of children as a driver of PC ownership may be declining (Cawson and Lewis 1999). Moreover, there is considerable evidence that the gap between those able to use the Internet and those who are not Internet 'literate' is growing and may continue to do so as long as the PC remains the main access technology.

Until recently, surveys showed that many people reported that cost and lack of access were barriers to their use of ICTs at home. One significant factor in the rapid expansion of Internet usage was the introduction of Dixon's Freeserve in the last quarter of 1998 – this gave the company a 20% market share and there are comparisons here with the provision of free terminals in the 1970s, by Minitel in France. Perhaps most significantly, free (of annual or monthly fee) service providers are attracting new types of Internet users, generally older people from middle and lower income groups. Previously, users had been of a predominantly younger age and from middle and upper income groups (NOP Research Group). There are parallels with the introduction of pay-as-you-use mobile telephone tariffs, which have resulted in rapid penetration of mobile phones into new markets.

In the USA, the use of the Internet for 'e-shopping' has grown rapidly over the past few years, with new schemes to attract frequent shoppers – Netcentives and Clickrewards. The use of e-commerce in Europe is generally thought to lag two or three years behind the USA. However, in the UK, TescoNet and Virgin.net have been receiving increasing numbers of visitors: the Virgin homepage receives more than 6 million hits per month (Ody 1999: v). Moreover, trials of other electronic shopping devices such as Safeway's PalmPilots may also lead to new ways of purchasing basic items. The PalmPilot is a small hand-held electronic personal organiser that can be programmed using bar-code scanners, to store data about items recently purchased in the supermarket. It assists the purchaser in deciding which items to re-order, using a simple tick-box list. The unit can then be plugged into the telephone line to down-load the order to the supermarket.

With the rapid rate of growth in Internet usage it is difficult to predict the likely trends in interactive home technologies even one or two years into the future. The use of these technologies tends to change our traditional perceptions of space and time, breaking away from the limits imposed by physical boundaries of the home. Bill Mitchell argues that the Internet has a fundamentally different structure from more traditional physical forms of communication and interaction. It negates physical geometry, operating under quite different rules from those that organise action in the public places of traditional cities. For example an exchange of e-mail can link people at indeterminate locations. In contrast, in the traditional spatially defined city, 'where you are frequently tells who you are and who you are will frequently determine where you are allowed to be' (Mitchell 1995: 10). He argues that in this new world, the property industry's traditional rallying cry of:

> *... location, location, location becomes bandwidth, bandwidth, bandwidth – tapping directly into a broadband data highway is like being on Main Street... the bondage of bandwidth is displacing the tyranny of distance, and a new economy of land use and transportation is emerging ... in which high bandwidth connectivity is an increasingly crucial variable.* (Mitchell 1995: 17)

In this technological vision of the future, our homes would need to provide spaces that can be programmed for work, education, and entertainment. New forms of interactive space will be needed rather than the traditional rooms in which activities are dictated by the needs of various biological functions. Rooms could provide sites where:

> *... bits meet the body – where digital information is translated into visual, auditory, tactile, or otherwise perceptible forms, and conversely, where bodily actions are sensed and converted into digital information* (Mitchell 1995: 105).

Whilst these predictions may seem fantastical and even terrifying to contemplate, in the long run, it may even be possible to generate new living environments by automatically manipulating housing systems according to changing user needs. In the more immediate future, the *Smart Home* concept we wished to test would embrace a combination of applications relating to:

- safety, security and convenience in the control of household appliances;
- energy and environmental management;
- assistance and medical care for older people and those with disabilities;
- new forms of education, entertainment and business applications.

Applications would include home security and control over the domestic environment. These range from cookers, which automatically detect when pans are boiling over, to more effective management of heating and ventilation. Medical applications could include the provision of advice and remote monitoring or diagnosis of medical conditions. Memory-joggers could help people with learning difficulties, or mild forms of dementia. Technologies to summon help, such as pendant radio transmitters, are already widely used. *Smart Homes* may link these to other monitoring systems triggered by sensors. People with reduced vision could benefit from 'smart-cards' that could be programmed to switch devices on or off as the person enters and leaves the room. Automatic door entry or central locking could help those with problems in mobility or manipulation, as well as providing simple convenience when entering or leaving the home.

The use of these technologies raises many ethical questions from those concerning privacy and the degree of 'tele-surveillance' to issues relating to independence and control. The introduction of technologies which require registration for use or access, such as plastic credit cards, has resulted in widespread debates about the protection of privacy in modern society (Abercrombie *et al* 1986: 148-152). Nevertheless, they may also offer the benefit for more effective and efficient communication between those who need assistance and those who can provide it. This is potentially a boon for the increasing numbers of older people living alone and for resource-constrained health and care services.

For most people, *Smart Home* systems could simply offer additional convenience in everyday activities adding to the benefits provided by the two previous eras of technological change in the home, represented by the introduction of mechanical and then electrical technologies. However, we believe that digital technologies have the potential to offer more than this by providing an interactive window to the world outside, and by providing us with information and feedback that was previously impossible to obtain.

In the USA, about 50% of all households have a personal computer. Once PCs become commonplace in our homes it is possible that utilities companies, supermarkets, retailers, travel agents, local authorities and other providers will take advantage of delivering their services using new digital media. It is possible that most information, from paying bills to booking travel, will arrive and be transacted in our homes in a digital form. Bill Gates predicts that this will occur within the next ten years and that we will witness a shift to self-service digital transactions between businesses and their customers. Human involvement could shift from routine low-value tasks to high-value personal consultancy (Gates 1999).

CHAPTER 3

USER NEEDS AND MARKET NICHES

The future implementation of *Smart Home* systems will largely depend on the extent to which they offer improvements in the quality of life, solutions to actual household problems and reductions in occupiers' costs. There needs to be proven benefits and not burdens from their installation. At issue is how technology will affect everyone – young and old, those who are active, fit and healthy and those with illnesses and disabilities.

Many innovations fail to gain market acceptance because their design and function are not adequately aligned with users' real requirements, or they are difficult to use, with complicated interfaces. Sometimes, people simply do not want them, or they are incompatible with existing systems and customers are not prepared to spend the money necessary to re-equip their homes to accommodate new products. Other innovations fail because they have not been properly marketed and potential customers have little idea of the benefits on offer. They cannot see the point in spending their money on the product or service. Yet more fail because the price is too high for mass-markets to grow.

These difficulties have all contributed to the failure of mass-markets to emerge in digital home systems over the past 20 years. They represent different sides of a common problem: a poor understanding of user needs on the part of technologists, manufacturers and suppliers. Our earlier work on home automation in the UK and Japan identified these problems as barriers to growth in *Smart Home* markets.[1] For this reason, our efforts to develop the demonstration homes in York and Edinburgh began with a review of social, economic and housing policy trends affecting patterns of ownership and use, and the potential implications of these for *Smart Home* technologies. This work was followed by a detailed study of user needs, analysing requirements across different groups of people.

This part of the study presents the main issues emerging on the demand-side. In many cases there is simply no obvious demand. At this stage, people do not know what *Smart Homes* are and therefore have little interest in spending money on more technology or services, without clearly defined and proven benefits. We approached this problem from the perspective of analysing what current needs go unmet in the home, and assessing where gaps could possibly be filled by providing appropriate technologies and delivering new services. We begin by focusing on the changing nature of housing markets in the UK and assessing different attitudes to the home, and follow with a discussion on usability issues and the results of our user needs analysis.

❑ 3.1 Market composition

In 1996, there were more than 24.5 million dwellings in the UK. Of these, 16.5 million (67%) were owner-occupied, 4.6 million were rented from local authorities, 1.1 million rented from housing associations and 2.3 million were privately rented. Stock replacement rates are close to zero and the majority of new housing supplies the need for additional dwellings stimulated by demographic change and new household formation.

There is considerable latent demand for new housing in the UK. Projections of future requirements suggest that around 250,000 new dwellings are needed per annum for at least the next 18 years. Current output produces less than 200,000 new dwellings per year. Existing build rates are therefore too low to meet potential demand. Forecasts of new housing requirements indicate that the largest element will be for single people in the 30 to 50 year age range. Most will be owner-occupiers and wish to live in town houses rather than flats (Hooper *et al* 1998). In England, the number of 'married person' households is expected to grow by over 23% between 1996 and 2016, with the average annual increase rising from 43,000 to 272,000. The number of single person households aged 65 and over is expected to grow by nearly 31%, with the annual increase rising from 126,000 to 352,000.[2]

The dynamics of UK housing markets are therefore changing. Recent research by FPD-Savills indicates that younger buyers who traditionally moved most often are renting for longer and buying later. Moreover, there is a mismatch between people's aspirations and the quality of housing provided, such that there is strong demand for 'high quality' properties (in terms of their construction) and little interest in the rest (Spackman 1998). Furthermore, a recent opinion survey indicated that more than 83% would like increased flexibility, offering greater choice over initial design of their homes. Almost 80% wanted their homes to be more adaptable to accommodate changes in layouts at some stage during the use of their homes.[3]

In general, most people purchasing new homes make decisions about where to live and what type of dwelling to buy based on the criteria shown in Table 2.1. Issues of choice of layout, amenities and internal fittings are not such a high priority as location. Many people purchase housing that they believe will be easy to sell later, maintaining it as an investment. This tends to encourage conservatism in choice of aesthetics and design, inhibiting an interest in customisation which they perceive as detracting from the resale value.

Table 3.1: Criteria by which buyers of new housing make their choices

First-time buyer	Trading-up buyer
1. Price	1. Location
2. Location	2. Price
3. Internal amenities/size and number of rooms	3. The estate/external appearance
4. External appearance	4. Internal amenities
5. Quality of construction	5. Quality of construction

Source: Based on work in support of the Deputy Prime Minister's Construction Task Force, 1998, with thanks to Ruth Clifton, Ove Arup & Partners

Around 40% of all new private dwellings are built by the 25 largest housebuilders.[4] The majority of these producers focus solely on housebuilding and are no longer involved in other forms of construction activity. They compete for sales in a tough market place, which is generally segmented as follows:

- housing for first-time buyers;
- housing for those trading-up to larger family homes;
- executive housing;

- retirement homes – including a number of niche markets such as 'empty-nest' housing and private sheltered schemes;
- conversion and redevelopment schemes – such as conversion of offices into flats;
- self-procure and self-build housing.

Developers rarely include the types of products and systems one might expect in a *Smart Home*. They typically offer security systems and fire detection devices and sometimes entertainment systems in more expensive properties such as in executive housing. However, even in many of these we have found provision of only one telephone line, indicating that developers have not thought about future uses and requirements for multiple communications for telephone, fax and Internet connection. This contrasts with the USA, where there is now considerable interest by housing developers in providing appropriate cabling and communications connections. In some large urban areas, such as Dallas-Fort Worth it has been estimated that in 3% of all new housing in the Worth area, developers have installed a particular cabling system (Haddon).

UK private housing development is closely related to the value of land and profits accruing from returns on land development. Developers currently only take a short-term interest in the total lifecycle of the buildings they construct. Most construction work is procured from subcontractors specifically for each site. Moreover, British housing production is often slow, laborious and fails to deliver the choices found in other countries in Northern Europe, Japan or North America. Housing is expensive to run, difficult to maintain and often does not provide users with the functions and quality they expect. Housing repair and maintenance accounts for one quarter of total construction output and British people spend more than twice as much on fixing old and often out-of-date housing than they invest in new stock.[5]

In the UK, newly built dwellings only account for a small proportion of the total number of housing transactions each year – less than 10% of all sales, the majority being second-hand transfers. One reason for most people choosing to buy second-hand is that they gain more choice over location, and space standards are usually higher. New housing also tends to cost more than second-hand housing, although it is difficult to compare like with like in these calculations – see Figure 3.2. The type of housing produced is often not attractive enough to second-hand buyers to bring them into the new homes market, in spite of poor quality and low environmental performance in parts of the existing stock. There is therefore potential to capture a much larger share of the market by developing new and better products. It is possible that if new housing production were more competitive in terms of cost and quality its share of the total number of housing transactions could be significantly increased.

Housebuilders face uncertainty over what to produce and where to build, with growing environmental pressures forcing difficult choices about the use of green or brownfield sites. European directives are likely to promote increased levels of energy efficiency and reductions in greenhouse gases caused by heating new homes. Pressures are mounting to develop recyclable components and sustainable housing technologies. These issues could potentially add to the cost of development, exacerbating the differences between new and second-hand house prices. Perhaps for these reasons, the climate for innovation has improved, with a number of initiatives involving housing associations, developers, contractors, suppliers and the government working in partnership to increase standards and the industry's performance.

Figure 3.2: New and second-hand house prices

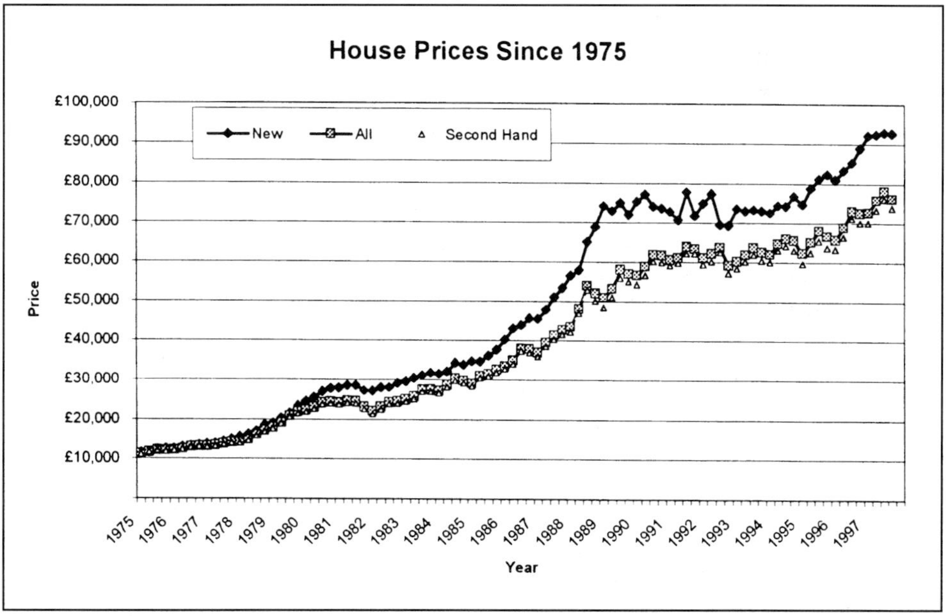

Source: Housing and Construction Statistics, DETR

Rented housing in the UK – particularly social-rented housing – has become stigmatised partly because of landlord and housing professionals' practices, and its treatment by successive governments. The social rented sector is perceived by many as the tenure of last resort, and in consequence people feel that they are either in temporary accommodation or have no sense of investment and ownership in their housing.

Social housing landlords are directly responsible for about 20% of all new dwelling completions. This sector has steadily moved from housing a cross-section of the community towards an emphasis on households who are unable to buy in the private market and to providing housing to support care in the community. In recent years the level of government funding received by social landlords has declined substantially, increasing their reliance on capital markets. This means that most smaller social landlords find it difficult to borrow for development and the majority of new dwellings are built by the 40 largest housing associations.

A fundamental problem when addressing the usefulness of *Smart Home* systems for potential users is the diversity of household types within the context of different market segments. A number of authors have attempted to segment the population in terms of household size and composition, social, employment and age characteristics to derive categories of needs and requirements relating to the possible use of different *Smart Home* applications. For example, Meyer and Schulze (1996) argue that there are nine household types (e.g. single-person households comprising younger or older people, family households, single-parent households), of which four have the most to gain from *Smart Home* systems:

- households in which both partners are employed;
- highly mobile, single-person households;
- families in middle age;
- older persons with limited physical abilities and disabled people.

Housing demand is often seen as an aspect of needs created through demographic change or the inability of particular social groups to gain access to adequate housing. However, pressure on the housing stock also arises from the way we use our homes. This is partly a function of demography, partly shaped by trends within the labour market and partly the result of attitudinal shifts. Additionally, developments in information and communication technologies clearly have the capacity to create demands from households for new services.

Many of the newly forming households will comprise elderly people, but an even larger number will comprise middle-aged single person households. The latter may well generate a growing demand for new tele-mediated consumer services, as well as having the economic capacity to invest in new *Smart Home* technologies. Growth in numbers of the elderly is also generating particular interest amongst technology suppliers and government.

❑ 3.2 Attitudes towards the home

Current experience with technologies in our homes, workplaces, travel and leisure activities creates a culture of understanding about what we are likely to accept by way of *Smart Home* systems. It also frames expectations of functions, usability and performance of future new technologies.

Changes in attitude to the way the home is used relate to the types of technologies installed in housing. Some have suggested that the purchase of a home may increasingly be seen as a lifetime investment, with first-time buyers delaying the decision to buy and existing owners remaining in their homes for longer. This may stem from increasing disillusionment over the financial benefits brought by owner-occupation and concern over insecurity in the labour market. There may also be a trend towards 'post-materialist' values, emphasising freedom to choose lifestyles, the aesthetic improvement of one's surroundings and desire to enhance intellectual ability (Ingelhart 1990; Abramson and Ingelhart 1995; Hirschman 1982; Wilkinson and Mulgan 1995).

The rapid growth in ownership of home-based leisure goods including PCs, video-recorders, fitness equipment, gardening, DIY etc. suggests that people's lifestyles have become increasingly home-centred. It is possible that these changes will translate into an even greater focus on the home as a centre – and, consequently, a demand for on-line services. However, over the next two decades the large growth in single person households, with a high propensity to consume new products and services, suggests there may be a growing demand for information and entertainment services and *Smart Home* equipment from this group.[6]

There is also a large and growing potential market for assistive technologies in the home. The market ranges from young people with interactive educational and entertainment requirements to the growing number of older people who have wide ranging health and care needs. Many people are also concerned about issues such as safety, security and energy use in the home. Requirements vary considerably depending upon the type of property and individual circumstances.

❑ 3.3 Changing work patterns

Another area of social change likely to have consequences for demand for *Smart Home* systems arises from the changing structure of advanced economies, driven by globalisation and intensified competition. This involves a decline in traditional rigid forms of employment and economic organisation and a rise in more flexible and responsive networked corporations. It has also been accompanied by a number of negative consequences, including the loss of jobs-for-life, and an increase in unemployment.[7] Associated with this is growth in the number of people setting up their own businesses from home, an increase in temporary employment in the service sector and what might be called 'information rich' economic.[8]

At a macro level it is possible to identify two types of employment decentralisation in the service sector: one geared towards the use of information and telecommunications technology to allow more flexible working for senior executives and professionals; and another for routine information processing jobs.[9] These have led to shifts in the division of labour between workplace and home, although progress towards mass teleworking has been far slower than commentators predicted in the 1970s. Using the home for work activities has certainly grown, but a more realistic view of teleworking involves individuals spending some of their time working at home, some in the office and some whilst travelling or wherever convenient.Teleworking involves a flexible combination of physical and electronic movements and spaces, rather than a total substitution of the physical by the electronic.[10]

Teleworking is attractive to employers because it offers them the chance to shift some of the costs of employing workers onto the home as well as potentially increasing productivity by overcoming the problems of lengthy journeys to work. This is likely to promote the continued rise in teleworking for routine activities where there is only a limited need for physical interactions with the office.[11] Employers' attitudes are changing and many will accept homeworking from freelancers, consultants and in cases when employees must largely work from home because of the need to care for an infant or older person.

Nevertheless, in spite of the much vaunted image of 'life on the Internet' the need for human proximity and social interaction remains. As Jonscher argues, people still go to the movies, pubs, cafes, and take holidays abroad. Face-to-face contact appears to be irreplaceable in the foreseeable future. Predictions of increases in power of computing and communication technologies are often understated, whilst those of its consequences for everyday life are usually overstated. We might have achieved the technical feat of wiring the planet – with more than 80 million km of fibre optic cable installed in the last 20 years – yet at another level, much less is changing in terms of our complex interactions in social and economic settings (Jonscher 1999: 248).

For the application of teleworking in housing organisations, see Grinyer, 1999.

❑ 3.4 An ageing population

That the population is ageing is incontrovertible. The number of households with members aged 65 or over will rise substantially over the next 20 years. An ageing population has implications for the housing market, particularly if the current housing stock is deficient in terms of meeting changing social, care and medical needs. These can be very wide ranging. Experiences of the ageing process and its ensuing social, care and medical needs can vary widely between the 'young' and 'old' elderly, and between elderly men and elderly women. Distinctions based on social class and ethnic group and on lifestyle may also be important influences on differing social needs (Cullen and Moran 1991; Taylor and Ford 1981).

As people get older they often experience multiple and increasing physical and sensory impairments. There is an increasing prevalence of health impairments and chronic illnesses amongst older people and this can have major implications for their housing requirements. The ageing process can make independent living, mobility, and the maintenance of social relationships considerably more difficult (Mollenkopf 1993). Nevertheless, most elderly people welcome the opportunity to remain in their own home (Smith *et al* 1993). Together, these factors suggest there will be a growing demand for appropriate servicing and adaptation of the existing housing stock to allow 'barrier-free' living – maintaining independence within one's own home.

Barrier-free or Lifetime homes can be created by relatively minor design modifications. The installation of digital control and communication systems represents the next stage on from changes to the physical environment and installation of mechanical aids. *Telecare* is an evolving field in which care, health and support services are partly provided for using new high-speed digital telecommunications infrastructure. Initial trials suggest that this can also offer possibilities for enabling greater independence in the home and overcoming isolation in the community (Gann *et al* 1998; Tang and Venables 1999).

The types of activities which could be supported include routine diagnostics, monitoring, screening, basic counselling and advice. Telecare offers a variety of benefits to users who can receive routine treatment almost immediately without travelling to, and waiting in surgeries; they can participate in routine monitoring and diagnostics which is less intrusive than traditional forms; or they can be assisted in routine treatments, including reminders about taking medication. The possibility of using *Smart Home* systems for continuous monitoring of people's health and wellbeing could increase the possibility of diagnosing changes in health status, automatically triggering an appropriate response from local community services or medical professionals. This can have benefits for both those with established medical conditions and those without. Single electronic records that can be held on smartcards, read by equipment in the home can be used as a means of transferring and updating medical records cheaply, as well as providing users with potentially greater control over sensitive information. However, the possible use of these technologies raises a number of financial and ethical issues. The latter arise from the increased capacity to monitor activities and resource deployment.

Concerns fall into two related areas. First, the extent to which housing providers, social services or health authorities could use new systems for random monitoring. For some, ethical concerns associated with monitoring people's movements within their homes, or recording the frequency of using the toilet or regularity of eating, could counteract the advantages of various *Smart Home* technologies for providing independence. For others, 'electronically tagging' a person with mild forms of dementia may give them increased freedom of movement without personal face-to-face supervision.

Second, questions have been raised about who benefits from *Smart Home* systems for older people and those with disabilities – the reassured relative, the relieved care staff or the person it is designed to help? Some applications can help to preserve individual dignity – for example when they obviate the need for help in the toilet or bath – and allow carers to provide a better quality of personal contact by removing much of the drudgery of caring. Furthermore, digital and physical aids offer the possibility of reducing management costs by providing remote access to dispersed homes and thus benefit users indirectly.

At all levels of dependency the option for older people to remain living in their existing homes is considerably cheaper than moving them to specialised accommodation. The economics of care provision may therefore influence government, health authorities and social services in decisions about whether to provide services remotely using telecare systems. This could increase demand for suitable *Smart Home* applications from individuals and households seeking to remain in their own homes. A number of specific activities could be serviced in part through the use of these systems including help for people with reduced vision and hearing, those with manipulation and mobility difficulties or with memory loss. Additional comfort, security and control of the domestic environment may also be achieved.

Within the next decade, older people are likely to become the new generation of Internet users – 'silver surfers'. This technology opens up possibilities for more involvement in running community activities and newsletters, managing businesses and charities, participating in lifelong learning and remaining mentally alert and active.

❑ 3.5 Home carers

The majority of help to frail and disabled people is provided by the informal sector. The main legislation underpinning the current form of provision was the National Health Service and Community Care Act, 1990. But 'care in the community' has been the dominant theme of government policy since the 1960s. This was regarded as both the best form of care and the most cost-effective. However, a large expansion of publicly funded private residential care has created pressure to find more cost-effective ways of caring (The Royal Commission on Long Term Care, 1999). Estimates from the results of the 1995 General Household Survey (GHS) indicate that there were about 5.7 million carers overall in Great Britain. Over the last five years there has been a consensus that this figure of around six million carers is not helpful for planning purposes (see Parker 1992: 17; and BMA 1995: 3).

The GHS estimates that in 1995 there were about one million carers in Great Britain who were looking after dependants for more than 20 hours per week, and whose dependants could not be left for more than two hours. While anxieties have been expressed about the declining willingness or ability of families to support frail older people, there is little evidence to support this.

In the 1980s, supporting carers was seen as a highly cost-effective strategy to assisting delivery of care in the community. It was a means of providing care at a cost far less expensive than alternatives, although, as Twigg and Atkin (1994: 5-6) note:

> *The argument was rarely expressed in its most naked form, whereby the only reason to alleviate the circumstances of a carer was in order to ensure that he or she continued to give care.*

Respite care is mainly needed by carers who spend a high proportion of their time caring, and particularly by those who cannot leave their dependants for any significant time. In 1985, 24% of carers spent more than 25 hours a week caring. This fell to 23% in 1990, and then rose to 32% in 1995 (Rowlands *et al* 1998: 29, Table 22). On this basis, it has been estimated that about 1.7 million adults devoted at least 20 hours per week to caring in 1995, up from 1.5 million in 1985. It is from amongst this group that the main need for respite services arises. A most significant finding of the survey from our point of view is that 64% of carers spending at least 20 hours per week felt that they could not leave their dependant for two hours.

The use of *Smart Home* technologies offers prospects of removing some of the more mundane daily tasks of carers by facilitating new combinations of home care, medical support and remote care delivery. However, much work needs to be done to trial new combinations of delivery involving face-to-face and remote contact. New forms of care services might include reassurance and the provision of advice and routine monitoring using video links. Memory-joggers could also be helpful for some people with learning difficulties, or mild forms of dementia. Technologies to summon help, such as pendant radio transmitters, are already widely used. Some people wanted these to be linked to other monitoring systems triggered by sensors. Moreover, people with reduced vision could benefit from 'smart-cards' which could be programmed to switch devices on or off based on proximity.

The use of these technologies raises many ethical questions from those concerning privacy and the degree of 'telesurveillance' to issues relating to independence and control. Nevertheless, they also offer the benefit of more effective and efficient communication between those who need assistance and those who can provide it. This could be a boon for the increasing numbers of elderly people living alone and for cash-strapped health and care services. The introduction of *Smart Home* technologies for this market is, however, far from easy, as we will show in the next section.

3.6 Usability and *Smart Home* systems

There has been a general lack of research on issues concerning usability of *Smart Home* systems, particularly in the UK. To ensure that technologies are designed to perform in a useful way with user-friendly interfaces, expertise from a number of different disciplines is required, at concept and prototyping stages, including: ergonomic, psychology, occupational therapy, sociology, economics and other specialist inputs. Equipment and systems testing in the *Domotique* laboratory in France has shown the benefits of this type of prototyping. Work of a similar nature has not been carried out in the UK.

As well as technical and funding problems, there are a number of social barriers to the introduction and diffusion of the technologies discussed above. These are partly related to attitudes and awareness on the part of user groups and carers, and partly to concern over ethical and privacy issues such as increased monitoring or the potential for greater isolation of individuals arising from remote service provision. To a large extent, however, these cultural and social barriers result from a lack of user input into the design process and lack of systematic empirical evaluation of these technologies.

Involving real users in the design of *Smart Homes* projects and in the evaluation process is critical to the development of new technologies (Keinonen 1994). Involving users ensures there is an appropriate analysis of their requirements and design solutions. User participation also promotes a sense of ownership, commitment and understanding of the design solutions. Failure to involve users can lead to products and services which are poorly matched to their requirements, and which seriously under-perform from a user perspective. In the long run this is likely to result in persistent disappointment with new technologies and financial costs arising from poor market take-up.

Product usability is a relatively new factor in industrial design, which has traditionally sought to support engineering and marketing by improving the physical appearance and feel of products. In traditional design, usability has largely been concerned with ergonomics, embodying in physical forms, knowledge about how people use artefacts (March 1994; Devries *et al* 1994). However, user-centred design also needs to encompass the cognitive aspects of using products and services, for example, issues of logic and how people feel about using them. Designing products in such a way as to eliminate fear of using them, and making them engaging to use, involves building in a combination of simplicity, ease of use, as well as offering distinctive value to customers.

User-centred design therefore requires the integration of knowledge from sociology, anthropology, computer science, cognitive psychology, visual design and ergonomics. Designing usable systems raises a number of issues, including the need for manufacturers to acquire knowledge about:

- *Who will use the system* – the physiological and psychological capabilities of users and their socio-cultural characteristics. This relates not only to the specific characteristics of a given user population and individual users, but also to universal human characteristics;
- *What it will be used for* – repetitivity of tasks, variability in nature of tasks, skill/knowledge requirements of tasks;
- *The context and environment in which it will be used* – physical conditions, health and safety;
- *What is technically and logically feasible* – costs, development timescales, building constraints.

(March 1994; Preece 1993)

The number and diversity of the potential users, the variable context in which products and services are used, and the need for manufacturers to balance usability and other design goals, make the aim of user-centred design complex. Using interviews or rank order techniques to ask direct questions aimed at exploring consumer requirements can be difficult because of problems in developing instruments which allow people to talk about commonplace, obvious or routine issues. This makes it hard to investigate the way technology that is integrated in everyday life (household appliances, TV, telephone, etc.) is used. More significantly, it is difficult to develop survey instruments which investigate people's use of products and services *that have yet to exist*.

Workshops and focus groups can help tease out common problems or wishes, and elaborate on areas that may not arise in individual interviews or surveys. They can be particularly useful because they allow users to exchange ideas on a 'peer to peer' basis, whereas in other experimental or observational evaluation procedures 'experts' frequently outnumber users and tend to set the agenda themselves.

In many consumer goods industries, these problems have driven manufacturers to spend more time testing products and concepts in the actual context of use, although this as yet does not appear to be the case in many *Smart Home* applications. The objective of in-use testing is to investigate the utility, usability and acceptability of products and gather information on possible corrections and improvements. Performing usability tests poses a number of problems, though. Research in Human-Computer Interaction (HCI) can shed some light on the processes and problems of evaluation (Bannert and Kunkel 1991; George 1995; Hix 1993; Shackel 1984). In particular, decisions need to be made about:

(1) *When* to do the evaluation. Evaluation can essentially be carried out at two stages:

- before implementation, in order to influence the product (known as 'formative evaluation'); or
- after implementation, to test the functioning of the product or system ('summative evaluation').

(2) *How* to do the evaluation. This can take the form of:

- analytic evaluation, using formal or semi-formal interface descriptions to predict user performance (this tends to be used early in design cycles);
- evaluation using experts to assess an interface (this lies between theoretical approaches and empirical methods);
- observational evaluation – monitoring or observing users' behaviour when using the product or system (this involves real users, with no task restrictions);
- survey evaluation – eliciting users' subjective opinions;
- experimental evaluation – using scientific experimental practices to test hypotheses.

(3) *Which* usability areas to test and *what* measurement indicators to use. Key considerations are:

- ease of use – whether the application can be correctly used first time; time taken to learn to use; success rate in meeting the specified range of users, tasks and environments;
- effectiveness of use in terms of performance – number of problems occurring each time the application is used, their nature and cause;
- user satisfaction with ease of use – judgements about convenience, comfort, effort, satisfaction.

Issues of ease-of-use are very important in terms of building customer confidence in new technologies. People need to feel that 'they are all right with this new little device'. They need a sense of security that they will understand how to operate it, not just in everyday use, but in case something goes wrong – the sense of 'relief' offered by being connected to a source of help through simple 'alarm-call' systems is a case in point.

Failure on the part of product and service designers to undertake rigorous evaluations such as those described above is one of the reasons why *Smart Home* systems have not been developed to meet users' needs. Another problem is that many systems and products probably require producers to invest in training and familiarisation programmes to help people get the most out of their systems. Most evaluations have been made outside the UK. One study, carried out in 1992-93 by the Helsinki University of Art and Design, found that evaluating the following key variables was critical for achieving user-friendly interfaces:

- the number of visual elements and the impression of reality of the representation – more figurative interfaces were preferred;
- the functional layout of buttons and close connections between buttons and related labelling – the use of a compact keypad with few modal buttons and a separate display can cause users major difficulties;
- the fact that users did not make use of textual information on a screen apart from one button label at a time;
- a style of interaction which involved separate phases for initialisation, editing parameter default values without immediate response and explicit approval commands, was poorly understood by elderly users;
- improved control over home systems by elderly users can be achieved by the user helping to design master commands.

(Keinonen 1994)

Meyer and Schulze (1996) argue that since women remain responsible for the main burden of domestic tasks, the acceptability of *Smart Homes* technologies is also related to their attitudes towards innovation. Acceptance will therefore vary by household type, notably its size and composition, internal division of labour and stage in the family lifecycle. Certain types of households have the most to gain from implementing integrated *Smart Home* systems. These include: households in which both partners are working, highly mobile single-person households, and those with elderly people or people with disabilities.

❑ 3.7 User needs analysis at Edinvar and Joseph Rowntree

A number of focus-group meetings and discussions were held with residents and carers at Edinvar and the Joseph Rowntree Housing Trust, using a standard semi-structured questionnaire checklist to elicit views and opinions about residents' needs and the potential benefits of using *Smart Home* systems. Problems were experienced in explaining what we thought was meant by *Smart Home* systems to people who had never heard of the concept or technology. This highlighted the need to build demonstration homes or customer experience centres – along the lines of those found in Japan (Palmer *et al* 1998) – in which technologies could be piloted.

Among the main features emerging from our user-needs focus-groups was a desire for *Smart Home* systems to address the needs of residents in the following areas:

- safety, security and convenience in the control of household appliances;
- energy and environmental management;
- improved internal and external communications, including access control in and out of the home;
- assistance and medical care for older people and those with disabilities; and
- new forms of entertainment and business applications.

Requirements varied considerably depending upon individual circumstances. They included door entry systems, home security and control over the domestic environment such as automatic lighting or the possibility to control motorised window and door openers. Automatic door entry or central locking could help those with problems in mobility or manipulation. Others required cookers which automatically detect when pans are boiling over, and some wanted more effective management of heating and ventilation.

The principal problems residents and carers wished to see addressed, and the possible implications, are summarised in Table 3.2.

■ Access

Access to the home itself (opening and closing doors) and receiving visitors (identification, letting them in/out, checking door is locked) can be problematic. Access problems can also arise within the home because residents leave hard to manipulate doors open or they lose keys.

Carers at the JRHT scheme had some concerns about the awkwardness of some doors for mobility impaired residents. While there was interest in the possibility of remote controlled door entry systems, with a control on the zimmer frame or wheelchair, it was also pointed out that too many automatic doors, security systems and 'lifetime' homes access facilities can deter potential residents. These facilities were therefore more likely to be acceptable in bungalow accommodation than residential homes.

Shop- or library-style exit gates to warn residents they have left their keys behind is a possible feature, highlighted by the Edinvar carers and residents but not the JRHT interviewees. The latter felt that problems over residents forgetting or losing keys could, however, grow as the age profile of the scheme changed.

Interviewees at both schemes felt that their current voice-only entryphone systems are hard to use for people with hearing difficulties. There can also be problems for people with restricted mobility in reaching the entryphone when visitors arrive. Some residents sometimes found it hard to remember how to use the system. These problems could to some extent be alleviated by video-based entry systems – perhaps connected to the resident's TV set and the use of some form of 'silent bell', such as flashing lights. Video systems could have the further advantage of allowing residents to monitor visitors and reduce their fears of unwelcome visitors.

Table 3.2: Edinvar and JRHT residents' and carers' *Smart Home* requirements

Problem area – carers	Problem area – resident	Possible solution	Issues
Access problems • Awkward doors • Loss of keys • Inadequate entryphone systems	*Access problems* • Awkward doors • Loss of keys • Inadequate entryphone systems	• Remote controlled door entry systems • Shop-style exit monitoring • Video entryphones	• Too many automatic doors • Security systems and 'lifetime' homes facilities can deter potential residents • Ethics of monitoring human movement • Ease of use
Identifying and acting on abnormal situations, e.g. • Fire • Water leaks • Windows open • Power off	Discontentment over smoke detectors	• Improved and centralised monitoring systems • Automatic cut-out for cookers • Better identification of switches	• Ease of use
Security problems • Leaving windows open or doors unlocked on exit • Identifying visitors • Medical emergencies		• Central locking system • Lighting systems connected to front doors • Monitoring systems to locate residents when alarm raised	• Ability to override centralised systems • Ethics of remote monitoring
General comfort • Alert to inadequate heating • Night-time confusion when going to bathroom • Confusion about what appliances are switched on • Problems using washing machine	• Confusing individual room heating controls • Unsophisticated pre-set water temperature control in bathroom • More sophisticated washing machines & indication of completed washing cycle	• Easy to understand energy management system • Remote monitoring of central heating • More advanced water temperature control system • Lighting system to light path to bathroom • Centralised monitoring of domestic appliances.	• Need to avoid deterring people from using their central heating because of concern over its cost • Ease of using equipment and programmes
Improving the internal communications system	Improving the internal communications system	Interactive TV and video links	

■ Safety and security

Safety and security problems largely relate to fire hazards from kitchen and other appliances, rather than the threat of external intruders. There was a high level of discontentment over the existing smoke detectors in both the Edinvar and JRHT schemes. These were felt to be poor quality and inaccurate. Some interviewees suggested that carers should be able to check centrally whether alarms were 'live' or not. It was noted that there was resistance from some informal or family carers to residents doing their own cooking because of concern over kitchen hazards. Other safety concerns relate to the provision of cues to allow better identification of switches.

These issues point to the need for systems which warn of appliance breakdowns or misuse, such as detection devices and automatic cut-out systems to prevent pans boiling over or over-heating, or alarms which detect when the fridge has been accidentally switched off. There was also felt to be a need for cues which tell residents that electric hobs are switched on. However, interviewees were concerned about the cost of such facilities in cases where residents owned their own cookers and other electrical appliances.

Carers suggested that it might be useful to introduce systems which allowed them to remotely check whether cookers had been turned off and windows closed when a resident left the building. The introduction of some form of central locking system, with an emergency override for carers, was seen as potentially beneficial, as were lighting systems connected to front doors or which light up paths from the main door to individual doors.

Carers also saw potential benefits, as well as ethical problems, in forms of *remote monitoring systems*. Of particular concern was the ability of carers to determine the location of residents when an alarm was raised. Video monitoring, infra-red detection or pressure pads were felt to offer advantages, although there was concern over the ethics of monitoring residents' movements.

■ Environmental control and central control of appliances

Some tenants found the individual heating controls in each room confusing and would consequently switch off the entire system. This suggested that it may be useful to introduce an easy-to-understand energy management system which could not only ensure that residents are able to make adjustments easily to the heating controls in each room, but also provide an indication of energy use. Some residents and carers were, however, concerned that too much information on energy use might deter people from using their central heating because of concern over its cost. Nevertheless, remote monitoring of central heating by carers could provide indications of inadequate heating. JRHT interviewees pointed out that although there were now fewer disconnections by utilities for non-payment of bills, there had probably been an increase in 'self-disconnection', the voluntary non-use of heating.

In the bathroom it was felt that the current system for pre-set water temperature control was not sophisticated enough and an advanced water temperature control system was needed. This should allow users to pre-set personal temperature parameters.

Improved, user-friendly lighting systems, which light the path to the bathroom or toilet were also seen as useful for helping residents who sometimes wake up confused in the night. Some interviewees felt that dimmer switches were not as important as systems which allowed residents to remotely switch from main to side lights.

Although some residents felt that the centralised switching of appliances could be beneficial, there was not much interest in systems to allow monitoring of appliances via the TV. However, carers felt that some centralised monitoring of domestic appliances would help to overcome problems arising from residents' confusion about what is switched on and consequently switching all appliances off. Simpler programmes on washing machines was seen as a key improvement, along with some form of mechanism to inform people with reduced sight when washing cycles were completed.

■ Improved communications

There was considerable interest on the part of carers and residents in the possibility of improving the communication systems, perhaps through use of interactive TV and video links with carers and other residents.

❑ 3.8 Issues for the development of *Smart Home* systems

As we have noted, a fundamental difficulty when addressing the usefulness of *Smart Home* systems is the diversity of households types and needs. This raises questions about the kinds of conclusion that can be drawn from the JRHT and Edinvar demonstration projects. Both of these will be used by residents with a range of social and physical needs, and differing learning capabilities.

Testing products and concepts in the context of use raises questions about when to do the evaluation (before or after implementation), how to do the evaluation (there is a wide range of approaches), which usability areas to test and what measurement indicators to use.

The best methods for carrying out post-implementation evaluation are likely to include a combination of observation – monitoring or observing users' behaviour when using the product or system – and survey work to elicit users' subjective opinions. Usability can be tested by measuring a number of indicators, for example, to collect data on whether the application can be correctly used first time, how long it takes to learn how to use it, and the number of problems occurring each time the application is used. Users' judgements about convenience, comfort, effort, and satisfaction can be collected.

Notes

1 See Gann 1992b; Gann *et al* 1994; and Gann *et al* 1995

2 In 1996, nearly 188,000 new dwellings were completed in the UK, of which 153,400 were built for the private sector, 32,500 for housing associations and the remainder by local authorities (*Housing and Construction Statistics*, DETR). Figures on growth of single person households come from DOE 1995.

3 The survey of 1000 people was carried out by 2000 Homes at the 1998 Evening Standard Home Buyers Show. Further details are available from: 2kh, 108-110 Judd Street, London, WC1H 9NT.

4 See Barlow 1999.

5 In 1996, the value of work carried out by British contractors producing new public and private housing was £7bn compared with £15bn in repair and maintenance (at current prices; source: *Housing and Construction Statistics*, DETR).

6 Although a survey conducted by Haddon *et al* (no date) recently found that products and services ranked low by consumers included systems which take over household budgeting and ordering, and systems linked to enhancing entertainment.

7 See Sennett 1998

8 See Castells 1998; Dicken 1992; Hepworth 1989; Knight and Gappert 1989
9 See Graham and Marvin 1996
10 See Hillman 1993
11 See Graham and Marvin 1996

CHAPTER 4

SPECIFYING *SMART HOME* TECHNOLOGIES

The previous two chapters of this study explored issues concerning the use of technologies in the home, together with technical, economic and social drivers and constraints to the adoption of *Smart Home* technologies. User requirements and housing markets are changing. At the same time, digital technologies and the functions and services they facilitate are evolving at a rapid pace. *Smart Home* systems, and many of the variables within which such technologies can be deployed are therefore changing rapidly, making it difficult to determine what systems to specify and how much should be paid for them. This chapter aims to make sense of technologies for automating activities within the home and emerging interactive communication systems, their potential uses and the benefits they offer. It draws upon experience of specifying systems for the two demonstration sites, in York and Edinburgh. It also questions a number of common perceptions and assumptions about the ways in which systems are configured and integrated and the role of international standards. The main functional activities and requirements are aligned with particular technical solutions. Finally, a simple, generic specification for *Smart Home* systems is provided.

❑ 4.1 Towards automated, informational homes

Earlier we provided a number of insights into the ways in which the diffusion of Information and Communication Technologies (ICTs) are changing social and economic activities, the ways we organise life at home and the domestic environment itself. These technologies embody a number of generic qualities, which, if organised in the right way, can improve quality of life and the provision of new services. In particular, they can assist in activities which have hitherto been constrained by the need for physical and/or temporal proximity – the need to touch a machine to turn it on or off, and/or for it to operate whilst one is present. Digital communication and control systems in theory permit users better command over their own space and time, by storing and acting upon pre-programmed information. The ability for individuals to programme software in systems and equipment is important in this context.

These attributes may provide new opportunities for automation in the domestic environment. Automation can range from:

a) simple fixed applications with pre-defined and pre-established operations; through

b) programmable applications and devices; to

c) fully flexible and automated applications and networks of devices sharing information and providing it to consumers.

But ICTs may enable more than simple automated functions, by generating their own information about product, environmental or service performance. The ability to present and transmit information in digital forms – whether by telephone, radio, television, email, or around a circuit (bus system) in the home – has the potential to alter radically the ways in which we use information at home; especially when considered from the viewpoint of traditional printed matter. Such technologies offer the potential to introduce new interactive information services, transaction services such as on-line banking, invoicing and bill-paying, teleshopping, and messaging services including electronic mail. Service providers can now be located outside the local community, hence telecommunications technologies have an important role to play in the development of network based services to, and within the home.

The notion of 'informating' processes was first explained by Zuboff (1988) in the context of changes occurring in the workplace due to the introduction of Information Technology. However, the concept has equal relevance in the domestic environment where it is possible to organise systems in such a way that they provide users with improved information, not previously available: for example, on energy usage, about callers and visitors or self-diagnostics of faulty equipment. Some systems can even 'learn' repetitive functions or actions, adapting internal environments to suit different occupants' requirements – intelligent fridges which alert users to food which has gone beyond its use-by date is one example. This property of ICTs – to enable new knowledge to be created about processes and events – particularly when coupled with the use of new external information services, may provide new opportunities for improving the ways in which people manage family and professional life. This is what we call the 'informational home'. It has the potential to offer users far more flexibility and value than traditional automated functions. In order to understand how these systems might work in the domestic environment it is necessary to differentiate between different types of information processes. Table 4.1 illustrates the main processes which need to be considered in the design of *Smart Home* systems.

Table 4.1: Types of information processes and activities in Smart Home systems

Types of process	Types of activity and technology
Production of information	Sensing, creating, monitoring and informating devices
Storage and retrieval	Interfaces and accessing systems
Transmission and receipt	Communication systems
Transforming	Computing and manipulation devices
Relating and displaying	Presentation, interface and display equipment
Acting on information	Alarms, prompts, actuators and motor devices

Source: adapted from Miles 1988: 7.

Many people reading this may feel fearful of the unknown consequences of technology, or the potential loss of control over their home environment. Whilst such fears may be justified by contemporary experiences with ICTs, *Smart Home* technologies can be designed and engineered to enhance individual control over the home environment. People are good at processing knowledge and making decisions in uncertain environments, whereas computer systems are useful for handling large quantities of routine, standard data. Moreover, communication networks can enable computers in different systems or components to respond to one another. It is much more difficult, if not impossible, to automate what we do with our minds in comparison to what we do with our hands (Jonscher 1999). Yet, if *Smart Homes* can be designed to harness the best from all three domains then they may provide real benefits to everyone using them.

It was with these ideas in mind that a specification was written for systems for the demonstration sites in York and Edinburgh. We wanted to find out what routines could be assisted in the home and what information could be collected which was not available before the use of ICTs. What technologies are available and how might they be used? Table 4.2 illustrates a number of examples of key *Smart Home* technologies and systems. The pace of technological change is rapid and this list therefore remains necessarily incomplete. Moreover, we have omitted many specialist systems and items of equipment such as those classified within the field of telecare and telemedicine. These are the subject of a forthcoming report (see Gann *et al* 1999, forthcoming).

❑ 4.2 Do we need integrated systems and international standards?

For the past two and a half decades large consumer electronics companies, electrical equipment manufacturers and to some extent, utilities companies, have been developing systems and components for use in the home. These have relied on the development of digital technologies to facilitate a variety of functions, and the ability to integrate systems. There is nothing new about the enabling technologies upon which the notion of the *Smart Home* has been developed. Key technological developments underpinning these systems include the replacement of electromechanical switching by digital switching, and traditional twisted pair and coaxial cables by optical fibres in long-distance telephony and the capability for bi-directionality (two-way communications) and developments in end devices such as 'Web TV' and video phones.

Broadly, these developments allow the integration of household functions within homes and between homes and outside services. The ability to communicate and control lies at the heart of these systems, and it is often believed that it is necessary to integrate systems in order to provide the types of functions that people will want to use. Combined in the right way they may achieve the goal of increasing functionality in the home. Figure 4.1 shows a number of levels of systems integration en route to the fully automated, informational *Smart Home*.

In this representation, equipment manufacturers and systems suppliers from different industries are shown to be converging to reach the ultimate goal of integrated home systems. Telecommunication companies, water, gas and electricity suppliers and building services (heating and electrical) firms are all developing systems to allow greater connectivity and the provision of value-added services. These include interactive and multimedia information services, remote energy management, and automated monitoring and control of domestic appliances. However, these attempts have generally failed to create the right conditions for the growth of mass-markets in *Smart Home* applications.

The integration of different systems is driven by attempts to provide new and better services to users, and to reduce costs. Costs can be reduced because it is possible to add more control points to digital systems at very little additional expense – the same system can be used to control lighting, security, heating etc. Traditionally these systems would be wired separately and users would control them from different devices. Achieving the same level of functionality in traditional hard-wired, stand-alone systems could therefore often involve expensive installation work. Their integration and provision over one cabling network with control from one device has the potential to reduce costs to users.

In some cases, the trend towards convergence of technologies has become so strong that what were traditionally independent systems can no longer be regarded as separate. The boundaries between different systems are becoming blurred because of integration. But systems integration can only be achieved through changes in the technological infrastructure – the provision of integrated networks and new software packages to run them. Changes in legislation such as fire regulations are also required if integrated systems are to be used.

Nevertheless, a number of reasons lie behind slow market acceptance of these products and realisation of supposed benefits of integrated systems in the home. For example, most commercially developed technologies are relatively expensive and tend to be aimed at middle and upper income homeowners, and there has been a narrow 'technology-push' approach, which fails to take adequate account of user needs. A third reason could reside in a poor awareness of the drivers and constraints to integration. Without an adequate number of proper field trials with actual users it is difficult to assess what functions need to be integrated together and which ones can remain stand-alone. The general drive towards systems integration therefore largely remains unchallenged and the costs and benefits of pursuing the type of

Table 4.2: Examples of digital control and communication equipment and systems in the home

Internal infrastructure: control and communications	**Interactive systems and external connectivity**
Wired or 'bus' systems: • Powerline • Twisted pair (inc. D.I.N. or Linkpower) • Co-axial • Fibre optic *Wireless 'signalling' systems:* • Infra-red • Radio	• Interactive/digital TV • Digital radio (RDS) • Telephone • Answerphone/voicemail • Home computer (email and Internet access) • Computer peripherals • Intelligent meters (powerline and radio) • Warden call systems • Medical diagnostic and monitoring equipment • Barcodes
Internal appliances, terminals and equipment	
User interfaces: • Television • Telephone (land line and GSM) • Computer and peripherals • Remote control handset • Door entry system • Voice activated equipment • Pressure switches • Touch-pads • Control panels • Digital watches with infra-red communication facilities • Personal data assistants, memory joggers (personal organisers) *Monitors and detectors:* • Passive infra-red (PIR) detectors and receivers (inc. microwave) • Thermostats • Smoke detectors • Alarms • Seismic sensors • Contact sensors • Iris recognition sensors • Medical monitoring devices	*Controllable, electric-powered devices and systems:* • Electric switches • Lighting • Ventilation equipment • Window openers • Shutters and blinds • Door openers • Cupboard lifters • Tap controls • Entertainment equipment (HiFi, video etc.) • Clocks • Security systems • Heating systems • Programmable white-goods (micro-waves, cookers and ovens, washing machines and dishwashers, fridges etc.) • Garage doors • Sprinkler systems • Pet-feeders

approach indicated in Figure 4.1 have not been adequately explored: do smoke detectors need to 'communicate' with video door-entry systems? Or will a simple battery operated smoke detector and door bell suffice?

Figure 4.1: From stand-alone systems and services to integrated Smart Homes

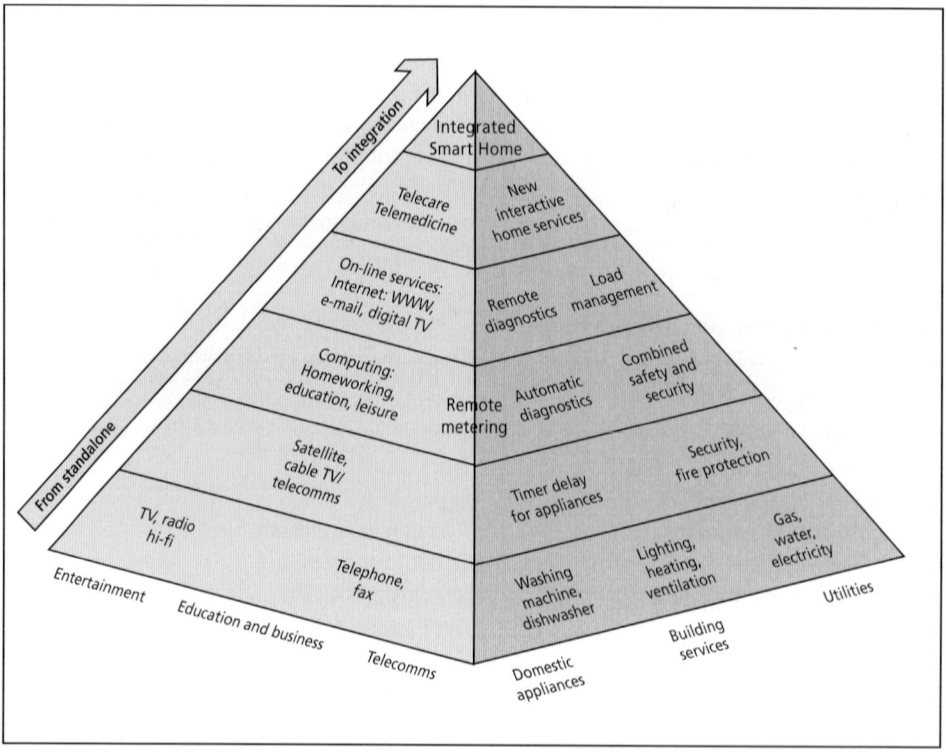

Moreover, equipment and appliances capable of receiving and transmitting performance data are required before integrated systems can be used effectively. Until recently there have been few domestic appliances produced for the European market that are compatible with any of the competing communication protocols. In spite of this, manufacturers have steadily increased the level of internal intelligence in their appliances providing, for example, time delays and performance monitoring. The capability of linking one appliance to another or to a wider home system has only just started to appear in products on the market. For example, Electrolux recently produced kitchen appliances with a variety of interactive and remote control facilities: including infra-red links between hob and extractor fan, enabling the fan to automatically run at a speed appropriate to the level of usage of the hob. The hob also has the ability to 'learn' the heat characteristics of pans used on it. In addition, ovens have been produced with remote control facilities, provided by the addition of GSM modules; and washing machines and dishwashers can interact with electricity meters to identify the cheapest times to run. These types of appliance are relatively new. Among the first to be able to exchange information with wider networks were released by Ariston Digital in March 1999.

Finally, integrated systems are unlikely to perform in a useful manner unless they have common interfaces, allowing users swift and easy access. Much research is being carried out on person-machine interfaces, particularly given the age and difficulties of use imposed by the main means of using computers – the QWERTY keyboard. It is possible that natural interfaces, touch-sensitive, voice recognition and/or eye-movement detection will be developed sufficiently for use in *Smart Homes* during the next decade. For example, a significant proportion of Microsoft's $2bn annual research budget is being spent on this and Bill Gates talks about developing computers which can 'hear you, see you and understand you' (Jonscher 1999: 216).

■ Standards

For devices to communicate – for example to share and exchange data about temperature readings – they must comply with the same communication protocols, speaking a common digital language. The issue of standard protocols has bedevilled information and communication industries over the last 30 years (Hawkins *et al* 1995). The concept of open systems standards is often espoused because they aim to facilitate seamless flows of information for software developers and users. There are three aspects: portability, scalability and interoperability. *Portability* aims to allow the same software to be run on different computers. *Scalability* aims to allow software to work on different sized machines. *Interoperability* aims to allow diverse hardware and software components to work together across networked systems.

For the past 20 years firms and industry associations in the USA, Europe and Japan have been working on the development of different standards to cover particular application areas and specify communication protocols. But attempts to develop standards have been painfully slow and generally resulted in cumbersome documents with little general agreement on the way forward. Partly as a consequence of this, mass-markets have failed to emerge and the use of *Smart Home* technologies has therefore been limited to those who could afford to pay for expensive one-off solutions, often based on security and entertainment systems.

The following features of protocol standards are of importance in the development of *Smart Home* systems: these are addressed in detail in Appendix 2.

- *Typical applications:* their history and development, including whether they are intended for use in homes, commercial buildings and/or factories.
- *Physical layer:* possibilities for using mains signalling (power-lines), copper wiring (including unscreened twisted pair, screened twisted pair, coaxial), optical fibre, cordless infra-red and radio technologies.
- *Main characteristics:* transmission speed (kbit/s), suitability for audio, data and video, topology, maximum number of devices on bus, maximum length, expandability, need for repeaters, and power requirements.
- *Compatibility:* with other protocols, with structured cabling systems, availability of gateways for interlinking systems, schemes for product certification.
- *Acceptance:* incorporation in European/international standards, adoption by manufacturers and users.
- *Ease of installation:* requirements for cabling and power, opportunities for using structured wiring, need for installation precautions (against electrical interference and for safety).
- *Ease of commissioning:* method of setting device addresses (hardware or software), availability of plug and play, need for user programming.
- *Ease of use:* quality of user interface.
- *Adaptability/expandability:* constraints imposed by power, cabling and network design, existence of third party suppliers of hardware and software, cost.
- *Reliability/robustness:* immunity to electrical interference, use of error correction, complexity of hardware and software, effect of heavy network traffic.

- *Security:* security of data transmission, suitability for use in safety-related applications (for example fire detection), data privacy.
- *Safety:* use of extra low voltage and any restrictions on use in bathrooms and outdoors.
- *Power requirements:* voltage, current, availability of power from bus.
- *Costs:* hardware costs per communications node, and of cabling; costs of system and applications software; costs of maintenance and upgrading.
- *Future developments:* in standardisation, adoption by market.

There are currently a number of competing standards for protocols and languages, which ultimately restricts the 'interoperability' of devices and systems. At the European level there is an agreement to achieve convergence between the three principal systems – EIB, BatiBUS, EHS – see Appendix 2. The goal is to establish common standards, a common system platform, compatible products and a unified approach to certification. Whether this will be successful remains to be seen since there are fundamental differences in the basic structure of the protocols and addressing mechanisms. Furthermore, other standards operate in the USA and Japan, and the LonWorks standard remains outside the converging model in Europe – see Figure 4.2. It is widely believed that LonWorks will become the de facto standard, as many companies are gearing up to provide this as an option to users. This will operate alongside the EHS system, which has the facility of carrying conventional analogue – not digital – video as well as control and information data.

Other ways around the problem of differing standards have been mooted, including adding a 'plug and play' (PnP) layer to existing standards or using the Internet as a communications medium. The Internet may offer the means for interoperability, although there remain problems since each device needs to be assigned a separate Internet address and linked to the computer network. Even if suppliers are able to develop these solutions, considerable support for systems integration and maintenance will still be required. Genuine PnP in personal computing remains elusive, despite the emergence of a demand driven market. It is likely to be a considerable time before it is possible for consumers to 'mix and match' components from different manufacturers of *Smart Home* systems.

Figure 4.2: Smart Home standards in the USA, Europe and Japan

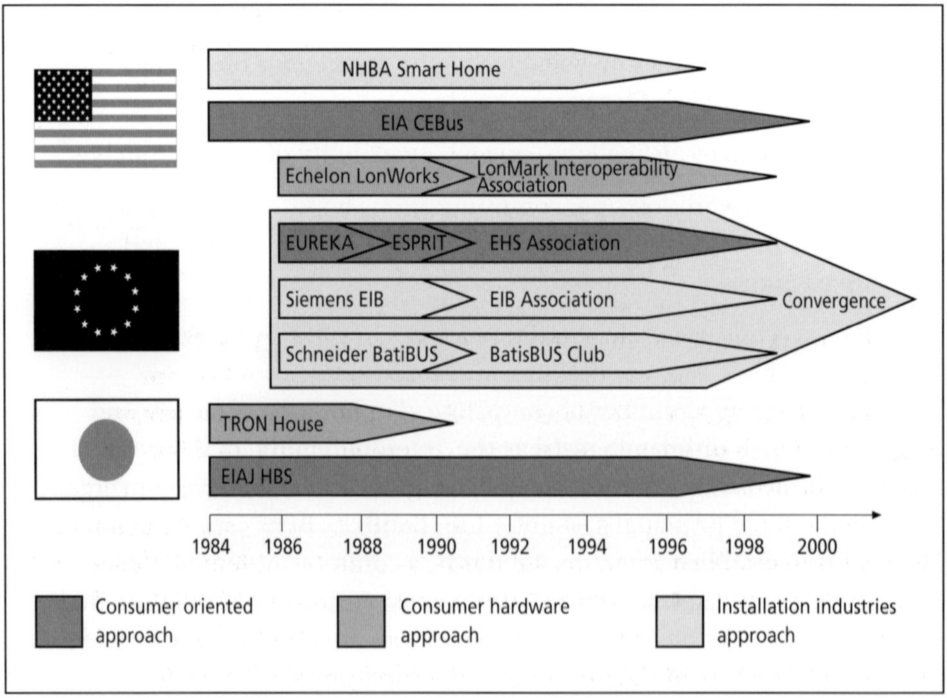

Source: Developed from Jeck (1997), Bromley (see Appendix 2), Heimer (1995).

❑ 4.3 Specifying technologies to assist in daily activities

Analysis with users in Edinburgh and York indicated two key areas for *Smart Home* application: internal environmental control, and home security, safety and emergency aid:

Internal environmental control

More sophisticated control of heating, ventilation and air conditioning (HVAC) involves the monitoring and control of the climate in individual areas of the home, permitting users to adjust the system to meet their own requirements.

Security and emergency aid

The development of new security systems involves more sophisticated sensors, alarms and user interfaces (Bedrosian and Bedrosian 1994). Integration with the telephone system could permit systems to be armed or disarmed remotely as well as enabling residents or operators to dial the home and listen for the sounds of an intruder. However, technological possibilities are in advance of what is usually found to be acceptable by police organisations and insurance companies, for whom remote arming and disarming of security systems is distinctly unwelcome. Alternatively, a recorded message can be sent to the resident or operator in the event of a fire or break-in.

Technologies used to *summon help* are also developing. While triggers such as button or pendant radio transmitter are common, new approaches involve increased use of sensors and remote monitoring to monitor the location of residents. In the longer term, researchers are investigating the possibility of 'smart rooms' (Pentland 1996). These may allow the recognition and interpretation of faces, expressions, sounds and gestures. Apart from identifying where people are, a smart room may help speed up the provision of help when it is needed.

The development of enhanced communication networks also greatly increases the capacity to monitor activities or resources. Systems comprising a series of sensors hooked up to a central data processor and sophisticated processing of information enable three types of 'flow' to be monitored (Dard 1996):

- *Human flows:* supervision of private and collective entryways, and spaces;
- *Energy flows:* monitoring of utility networks and calculation of energy in each residence;
- *Information flows:* managing the transmission and reception of messages between, say, carers and residents.

■ Functional areas

The technologies described above broadly address three functional areas relating to activities of daily living (ADL):

- assistive devices – including those for older people and those with disabilities;
- environmental adaptations; and
- labour-saving innovations.

Within the home a range of integrated and interactive systems potentially address specific ADL problems, but also raise a series of questions which have yet to be answered. These include how to create trust in the systems and prevent fear of equipment failure; how the system or service is paid for; and assurance that technical support services will be available. Furthermore, these systems bring together a variety of diverse technologies, which are at various stages of development, and it has yet to be seen whether or how they can be integrated.

Smart Home systems can be used to assist in every-day routine functions as well as assisting in meeting needs of people with a variety of different requirements. These include:

Reduced vision

This can be helped by good design of products and interfaces, including improvements in materials and lighting, and alternative input and output devices, such as speech recognition.

Poor hearing

This can be addressed by improved personal or group hearing aids, adjusting the voice signal or allowing an alternative medium to be used for telephony, subtitling in TV programming etc.

Manipulation difficulties

Many difficulties associated with manipulation can be addressed through design of basic mechanical aids and systems such as improved switches and upper limb aids (handrails and grab bars; general purpose hoists). However, digital systems also have a part to play, including voice activation systems and robotic arms.

Reduced mobility

Again, assistance is often best provided initially through the use of simple mechanical aids. However, digital systems can be used in lifting robots and sensor-guided wheelchairs.

Medical applications

These offer the prospect of removing some of the more mundane daily tasks of carers by allowing greater use of home health care and remote care. *Prevention* (e.g. automated screening) and *monitoring* (by self or remote diagnostic systems) are two options, as are improvements in access to information about services and memory-joggers, which remind people to take their prescribed medication (see Gann *et al* 1999 forthcoming for further details).

Table 4.3: Potential applications of technology and likely systems solutions

Potential application areas	Potential *Smart Home* designs and systems
General comfort and safety:	
Adequacy of temperature and ventilation controls	More sophisticated sensors, centralised monitoring of human movement
Fear of accidents and risks of injury	Fire and other alert systems
Fear of crime	Security systems
Mobility difficulties:	
Stairs	Adequacy of lighting in areas where falls are common Provision for lifting and mobility aids
Reaching	Accessibility and design of equipment and services, e.g. keys, handles, switches designed for access
Distances to shops etc.	Even and non-skid surfaces
Reduced strength and endurance	Equipment designed to use as little muscular force as possible Assistive devices, e.g. automatic door openers
Cleaning, routine maintenance:	
Recognition of cleaning need	In future, image processing and other dirt and bacteria detectors
Strength, mobility and endurance	Manipulation aids
Memory joggers and learning:	
Forgetting crucial daily activities	Monitoring household appliances
Learning new routines and activities	Help with night/day discrimination Reminders of appointments, social events, medication
Nutritional difficulties:	
Forgetting to eat; reduced motivation to eat	Identification of changes in eating habits
Problems with shopping, food preparation	Remote ordering of shopping
General age related changes:	
Reduced vision and hearing	Good design of products and interfaces – ergonomic, cognitive and emotional usability
Increased learning times, longer reaction times	Replace devices functioning on visual or aural abilities with other functional modes, e.g. tactile cues replace visual, acoustic cues replaced by visual cues Communication aids or non-vocal language skills to cope with speech impairment Reduced dependency on written instructions and communication, e.g. pictures rather than numbers on a key pad

Even if manufacturers succeed in generating more widespread understanding of *Smart Home* technologies, evidence from the early days of the personal computer industry suggests that a number of acceptance barriers will slow its initial adoption. These relate to consumers' concerns about:

- price stability;
- lack of information;
- standards compatibility across applications and when upgrading within specific applications;
- reliability, susceptibility to breakdown and foreseeable servicing costs;
- complexity in use.

Meyer and Schulze (1996) argue that acceptance will also vary by household type, notably its size and composition, internal division of labour and stage in the family lifecycle. Certain types of households have the most to gain from implementing integrated *Smart Home* systems. These include households in which both partners are working, highly mobile single-person households, and households containing elderly people or people with disabilities.

❑ 4.4 A generic, functional specification

In presenting the following general functional specification we have drawn on lessons from the above analysis of technical trends together with requirements from the user needs analysis discussed in previous chapters.

The general *Smart Home* specification has been developed on three levels – see Figure 4.3:

1. Basic infrastructure to accommodate general functions
2. Context specific requirements
3. User specific functions.

Level 1: the *basic infrastructure* is intended to be appropriate for use in any housing situation. This provides the backbone and central nervous system to which more context specific technologies can be added. The main decision at this level concerns the communication medium, for example, what type of bus system or power line communication system is appropriate. Choice of infrastructure has implications for all other decisions about what technologies can be supported, where they will be located and how they will be used. One of the most important decisions is which protocol to use for signalling and communication between devices. The basic infrastructure may also include a number of standard components applicable to all housing types regardless of form of ownership, location, size or value. The choice of basic infrastructure will also have implications at an organisational level for housing developers, social landlords, builders, and systems integrators, because it is likely to define the types of capabilities required for design, installation, maintenance and adaptation.

Level 2: *context specific requirements* for particular housing types. This is the level at which the basic *Smart Home* infrastructure is adapted to the particular installation environment in the context of different types of housing. It provides universal applications to be used by any occupant or visitor within the home. Choice of equipment at this level will also depend upon whether it is to be installed in apartments or houses and whether these are to be linked to particular service providers. Specification of general systems and equipment such as lighting controllers, alarm systems, and environmental controls could all depend on the size, position and intended types of occupancy of the dwelling. At this stage, the location of major pieces of equipment and cabling need to be defined.

Level 3: *user specific functions* provide features aimed at accommodating the needs of individual occupants. It is desirable that *Smart Home* systems should accommodate special features and performance criteria required by particular users. Where possible, this level should also accommodate portable plug-and-play devices and systems. For example, the ability to use particular, customisable interfaces can often assist in meeting specific user preferences. Familiarity with devices such as infra-red remote controllers makes these a general favourite although other interfaces have advantages to certain users, particularly those with special needs. Devices to support specific needs are also specified at this level: from assistive devices for the elderly or people with disabilities, to safety devices for parents with young children. Of equal importance is the way in which devices interact and this may also need to be specified by an individual user. This can generally be done once installations are complete, either by installers or by users themselves.

Figure 4.3: The 3-level generic specification

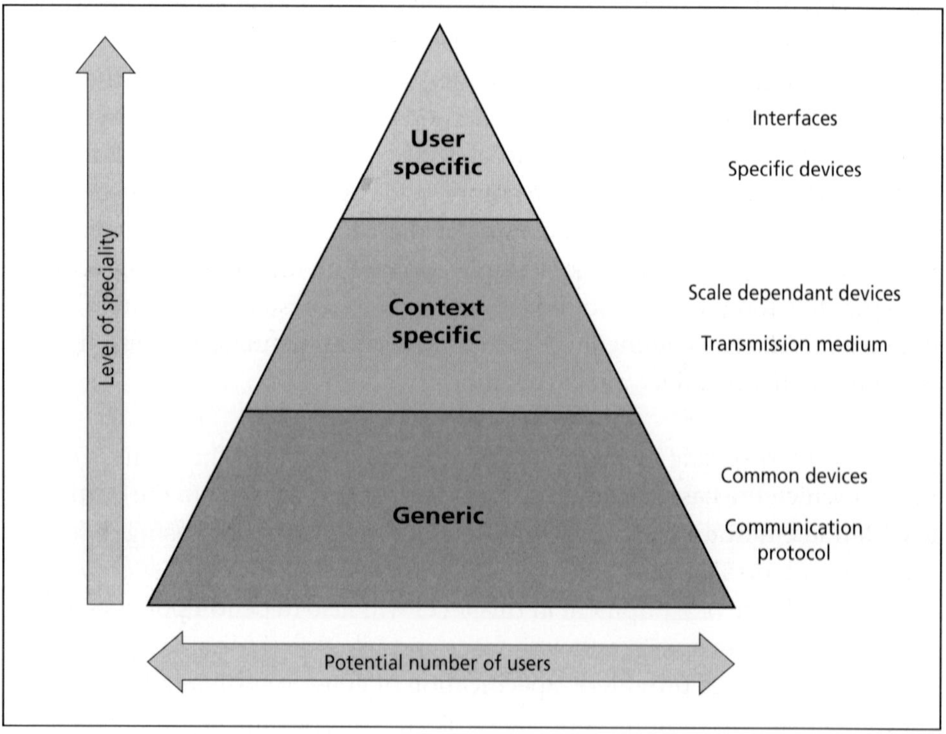

In addition, every level must satisfy a number of general conditions including:

Functionality The system must have clear and unambiguous functions.	**Ease of use** The system must be capable of supporting use by a wide range of different types of occupants, visitors and where necessary their carers. It must be safe and easy to use, assisting independent activities within the home.
Affordability The system must be inexpensive, with demonstrable benefits for individuals and housing providers.	**Replicability and ease of installation** The system needs to be available as a standard, reproducible product which has a low-installation impact and is easy to install in refurbishment and new build projects. Suppliers must be prepared to train for necessary installation skills required. →

Reliability and maintainability Manufacturers must indicate data on reliability, provide a full back-up and maintenance service, and where required train maintenance and operations staff.	**Flexibility and adaptability** The system must be programmable, accept add-ons and interface with other suppliers' equipment. Systems need to be capable of development as user needs change.
Upgradability The basic infrastructure must have a long shelf-life, it must be upgradable at low cost and effort.	**Interactivity** The system must offer wide interconnectivity and comply with recognised standards.

CHAPTER 5

IMPLEMENTATION: LESSONS FROM YORK AND EDINBURGH

> *Mitch was bored with being Ray Richardson's technical coordinator. He wanted to go back to being an architect, pure and simple. He wanted to design a house, or a school, or maybe a library. Nothing showy, nothing complicated, just attractive buildings that people would like looking at as much as being inside them. One thing was for sure. He had had quite enough of intelligent buildings. There was just too much to organize.* (Kerr 1996: 43)

Putting new ideas into practice is never easy. This part of the study describes the experience and lessons from designing, procuring, installing and operating digital systems in two demonstration *Smart Homes* in York and Edinburgh. It also raises issues about the rapid rate of technological change and the need to adapt or upgrade systems during use. Some of the issues discussed are necessarily of a technical nature and it is advisable for those not concerned with detailed technical design and integration to skip section 5.1. The main focus of activity was on the installation of systems to provide automation of simple functions within the home. The addition of new communication systems providing interactivity between the home and the world outside was not attempted in a systematic way in these demonstration projects.

The original intention had been to test benefits and constraints in two different installations: one, a new-build scheme, the other a refurbishment project. For reasons discussed below, this did not prove possible, and systems were eventually installed in a new bungalow in York, and a new apartment in Edinburgh. However, in practice, both represented retrofit projects because the dwellings had already been constructed before *Smart Home* systems were installed, although in the case of Edinburgh some provision for future adaptation had been made during construction. Two different systems and standards were chosen for demonstration purposes in order to make comparisons about design, installation and operation.

In terms of basic infrastructural requirements, there is a need for two types of data signalling around the home: low frequency or bandwidth, used to switch lights on or off, etc.; and high frequency for transmitting video, images and large quantities of data etc. *Smart Homes* need to be able to support both forms of communication. Installing new cabling can be expensive, time-consuming and disruptive. Existing electrical cables can be used to provide the means of communication for low frequency data signalling and, in theory, using these for data signalling can facilitate rapid installation with minimal disruption. However, they tend to be less reliable for high frequency communications and additional cabling is therefore often necessary.

In York, the Echelon-based LonWorks system and protocol was chosen to provide the basic, generic infrastructure. In this installation the intention was to use existing power lines as the main communications medium for control of devices. LonWorks is a control system which was originally designed to work primarily on a special communications network, or bus system, but also supports power line and radio signalling. It has been successfully deployed in office and industrial buildings.

In Edinburgh, the Siemens EIBus system was used to provide the generic infrastructure. This requires installation of a new cable network – bus system – around the building, on which communication and control signals can be passed. The system has been successfully used in office and industrial buildings and has also been used in a number of housing demonstration projects.

The project team learnt from the commercial office sector in which design, installation and commissioning were found to be critical stages in the construction of so called 'intelligent buildings' (Gann 1992b). Lessons show that most problems arise at the interface between one technology – or specialist skill – and others. Problems that had been identified in attempts to install 'intelligent building' systems in offices were found often to have their origins in errors occurring in design or in the supply chain. Three critical factors for success included:

- how the process is organised;
- single point management responsibility for the entire process;
- availability of appropriate skills, particularly for systems integration.

Moreover, successful installation of digital office technologies usually resulted when there was close co-operation between users and producers. The need for designers and systems integrators to understand users' demands was found to be important, although many users lacked the capability to draw up comprehensive briefs for their requirements. In the commercial office sector, it took time, and successive attempts at integrating systems in different projects, to improve the information flows necessary to achieve success.

A similar learning curve was thought to be needed in integrating digital technologies within housing. If lessons could be successfully captured from the prototype homes in York and Edinburgh they could provide participants and others with a significant step along the learning curve. This chapter describes what was learnt, starting with design and systems integration, followed by analysis of procurement and installation, including a discussion of costs and timescales. It concludes with analysis of different user perceptions of the demonstration projects, and a technical assessment of the two systems piloted.

❑ 5.1 Design and systems integration

Apart from a detailed understanding of different user requirements, designing *Smart Home* systems requires knowledge about technologies and systems integration, as well as how systems can be installed within the fabric of the building. Having drawn up specifications for the two sites, and held a workshop and briefing meetings with potential suppliers, it became evident that there were few organisations capable of integrating systems at an affordable price. It was therefore necessary to employ systems integrators directly in each housing association. In York, Colin Taylor, Chief Electrician at Joseph Rowntree Housing Trust took over the role of systems designer and integrator. In Edinburgh, Steve Bonner was recruited to Edinvar Housing Association to carry out these tasks.

The first lesson had been learnt: it was necessary to have significant, in-house technical expertise in order to proceed. Further resources had to be brought in to both demonstration schemes. In the current phase of technical development and market penetration, it is therefore difficult to conceive of how an organisation wishing to develop *Smart Homes* could do so, without investing heavily in training and internal technical capabilities. On the evidence of this project, the main lesson for housing providers wishing to install *Smart Home* systems is that they will need to invest in similar skills.

Resolving a number of other issues met during design and integration proved critical to the overall success of the two demonstration projects. Key lessons from the York experience are described in Table 5.1, perhaps the most important being the need to ensure interoperability between different, but supposedly compatible, components and testing this on a mock-up demonstration board. This allowed many sub-systems to be tested in laboratory conditions. For example, a system was built using Phillips lighting controllers, Zytron multi-sensor smoke, light and heat detectors and a speech unit. Frogability controls were used for door and window openers and Plumb Centre radiator controls were installed. MPS, Videx and Alarm Express systems were also used. Control of this system was tested using a PCTVnet television interface.

Table 5.1: Key events in the York project

October 1997 – the decision to use Echelon-based technology had been taken and Colin Taylor attended a LonWorks training course on Echelon systems. The majority of control equipment was ordered (Echelon LonPoints; Asgard cable spheres; Zytron smoke detection equipment).

November 1997 – a demonstration mock-up board was built to enable testing of equipment and experiments with different parts of the system to avoid disturbing the occupant in the proposed bungalow in which it had been planned to install the technology. Assembly of the board took 2 months part-time work, enabling a thorough familiarisation with technical matters.

January 1998 – the system appeared to work, but there were a number of problems: software for programming the system was only on beta (test) release. It had a number of inherent bugs that caused errors during tests and commissioning. This has now been resolved with the full release software.

Interoperability problems were experienced between Asgard spheres and Echelon network settings, which appeared to be incompatible. Echelon overcame the problem by modifying LonPoint and using this as the technical interface. Similar problems were experienced with some of the Zytron devices.

Construction of the demonstration mock-up board proved to have a number of uses, not least that it showed others what the project was attempting to achieve. It was used to assess the viability of using different types of equipment, illustrating how these could be of benefit in a real-life situation. Success at this stage convinced Joseph Rowntree Foundation, the main funders of the York project, that additional investment should be made to purchase more equipment for installation in the demonstration home. Experience with design and integration had caused a number of concerns over reliability and it was decided to make further trials before installing systems in the demonstration home, which at the time was a refurbishment bungalow in Lime Tree Avenue, York. Agreement was reached to build a second prototype demonstration board to include additional features.

At the same time, a new ceiling rose was designed to incorporate both input and output nodes and an Echelon compatible detection sensor – Figure 5.1. This product removed the need to use LonPoints at both switch and outlets of sub-systems and permitted control aspects of the system to be housed in a less obtrusive manner.

Figure 5.1: Specially designed ceiling rose, using customised Echelon input and output nodes

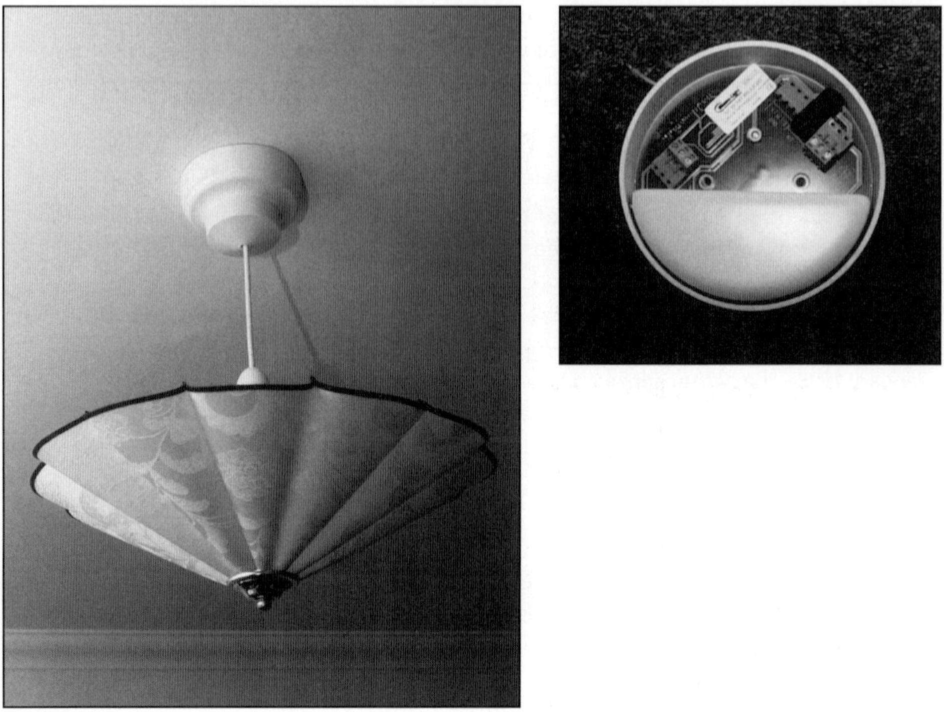

Unlike the York project, where a prototype system was mocked-up, work at Edinburgh proceeded with the intention of procuring a system for installation directly in the demonstration property. The main lessons from the early stages of the Edinburgh project are described in the following section. Further technical details and scheme designs for the York and Edinburgh dwellings are provided in Appendix 1.

❑ 5.2 Procurement and installation

Different issues arose at Edinburgh, the most significant being the need for suppliers to deliver equipment and provide adequate training and technical support on time – Table 5.2. Moreover, it was found that many of the components advertised by manufacturers were not ready. Some were still in prototype form and were not yet in manufacture.

An outline specification was developed and sent to a number of suppliers who were asked to provide tenders for supply and installation of equipment at the two demonstration sites. Tenders received were all more expensive than expected and fell well outside the remit for affordability. Moreover, most suppliers had difficulty in responding to the specific brief in spite of their previous statements of ability to supply. Delays occurred in choosing suppliers and time was spent checking suitability and capability. It became evident that in spite of much marketing hype and demonstration of technical competence in commercial office markets, no suppliers were able to meet the needs of the *Smart Home* demonstrators on their own.

The Edinburgh property, a flat at St Leonard's Court, was constructed in 1996, but the particular flat had never been occupied as it was ear-marked as a show-flat and for use in the trials. During construction of the flat, attempts had been made to build in flexibility for future changes anticipated in the development as a whole, and for the demonstration flat in particular. For example, cableways had been left behind skirting boards and conduit was installed under each door threshold in anticipation of the need to install *Smart Home* cabling – Figure 5.2. The cost of providing space for additional, future cabling in new housing or in major refurbishment work is negligible – less than £100 per dwelling on the Edinvar scheme. Issues concerning spread of smoke and fire through cableways and the likely implications for building regulations were not addressed, but they may have consequences in future applications of this type.

Figure 5.2: Provision of cableways in the Edinburgh flat

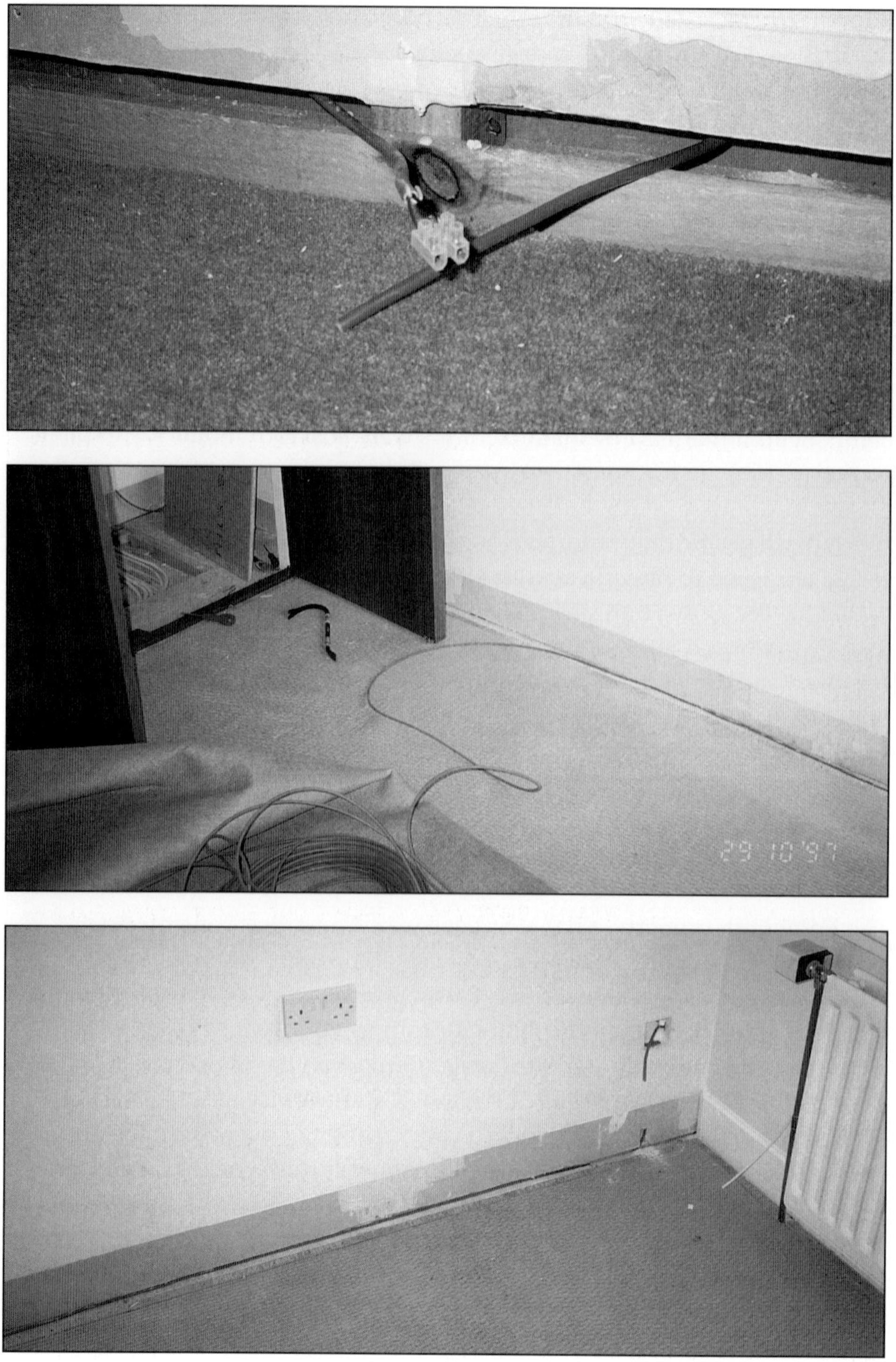

It became evident that installing cabling would be more difficult than expected, in spite of provision of cableways behind skirting boards and under door thresholds. The dwelling had been fitted out as a show flat and gripper rods used to fit carpets prevented skirting boards from being easily removed. In addition, routing of the radiator pipework hindered the use of intended cableways. As well as hindering the initial installation this was also likely to cause difficulties in future adaptation.

Table 5.2: Key events in the Edinburgh project

August 1997 – Steve Bonner was appointed to manage the project within Edinvar Housing Association. Siemens' InstaBus control equipment was ordered, based on a pared-down specification of the original requirements (reducing the expected cost from £10,000 to £5,000). Delivery was expected in early September. There was concern that the equipment ordered would prove insufficient to fully achieve the anticipated utility in the demonstration flat.

September 1997 – significant delays in delivery of Siemens equipment were experienced, but cabling was delivered to allow work to commence on installation. At this stage, Steve Bonner had not been able to attend specialist training and was therefore unclear about cabling requirements. Ideally, training should have been provided, followed by detailed design, equipment delivery and installation. It was not possible to achieve this at the time, because no training facilities were available in the UK.

October 1997 – Siemens equipment began to arrive and continued in a piece-meal manner throughout that month, making it difficult for consistent work to take place.

October through December 1997 – installation of the Bus and associated equipment. Original lighting circuits needed to be rewired from 2 ring circuits to 9 point to point circuits. Additional cableways needed to be installed in mini-trunking for equipment to be mounted at high level (such as passive infra-red sensors) and a number of doorways needed to be repositioned to accommodate door opening equipment.

All Bus wiring at this stage was installed on the premise that it would function in the same way as a 2 wire communications system as the only wiring guide available was an appendix to the product catalogue. Equipment installed by the end of December was set up to function as stand alone with no interoperability, although cabling and control equipment was fitted in preparation.

January 1998 – the first EIB (European Installation Bus) training course was held in the UK, attended by Steve Bonner. As well as learning how the system should be installed, the programming software was also made available to start introducing interoperability in the system.

January to March 1998 – other manufacturers' equipment is obtained requiring corresponding control equipment from Siemens. Previous problems in delivery by Siemens were not experienced on this occasion as orders were placed direct from Siemens, without using an electrical wholesaler, other than for processing invoices and payments.

March 1998 – Steve Bonner attended a visualisation software training programme (CNC Hub) which provided new skills to programme touchscreen controls for the entire system.

On the York project, timing of the development of the new Joseph Rowntree Housing Trust Hatrigg Oaks scheme provided an opportunity to carry out the first installation of the Echelon system. This was to facilitate demonstrations in a show home, permitting visitors to see the system working without disturbing residents. It was therefore decided to carry out a full installation on this site before proceeding with installation at Lime Tree Avenue.

■ Costs

Table 5.3 provides a comparison of costs for equipment installed in the two demonstration projects. In general, the costs appear prohibitive- around £1400 per room. They are certainly higher than a threshold of a few hundred pounds per room or a few thousand pounds per dwelling, which was our target to prove affordability. Costs are high in part because a wide range of equipment was installed which would normally be in excess of individual needs. But individual items such as light switches are also expensive when compared with standard, non-digital components. These costs are high in part because there is no volume market in which economies of scale come into play. Many components and systems were manufactured and sold for use in commercial offices, where volume of sales could provide bulk-purchase cost reductions and multiple devices could be controlled on the same system. Moreover, the savings made in large buildings are likely to provide a pay-back in areas such as energy saving, whereas these issues need further examination and research in the housing arena.

■ Time

The demonstration projects took much longer than planned. Reasons included difficulties in finding appropriate suppliers, the need to recruit and train in-house personnel and delays in delivery of equipment by suppliers. Such delays are perhaps to be expected in a research and prototype project and the formal project period was extended by 10 months.

Due to the fragmented nature of the work carried out and the piecemeal delivery of equipment for the demonstration projects it is not easy to provide a realistic estimate of how much time would be spent on each stage of a subsequent project. However, Figure 5.4 provides estimates of the time required to procure and install systems in a hypothetical project, based on data collected from the demonstration schemes.

Table 5.3: Comparative costs of installation at York and Edinburgh (£)

Joseph Rowntree Housing Trust (York)

Room contents	
Intelligent ceiling rose	110
Multi-sensor	70
Movement detector	45
Infra-red receiver	45
Intelligent plug	90
Window opener	240
Door opener	375
Curtain opener	195
Radiator control	40
Interfaces for the 4 above	180
Standard total per room	1390

		Alarm control	Video door entry	Gas detection	Warden call link	Computer interface	Power supply & controller	Cable, joints, etc.	Cupboard lifters	Total
Bedroom 1	1390	45								1435
Bedroom 2	1390	45								1435
Living room	1390	45	50		125	100				2610
Hall	1390									1390
Kitchen	1390			100			800	500	800	3590
Bathroom	1390									1390
Outside			210							210
Standard total	8340									
		135	260	100	125	1000	800	500		
									House total (ex VAT)	12,060

Edinvar Housing Association (Edinburgh)

Room contents	
Lighting control	129
Thermostat	119
Smoke/heat detector	140
Movement detector	91
Infra-red receiver	52
Intelligent plug	n/a
Window opener	200
Door opener	n/a
Curtain opener	600
Radiator control	70
Interfaces for the 4 above	inc.
Standard total per room	1401

		Alarm control	Video door entry	Gas detection	Warden call link	Computer interface	Power supply & controller	Cable, joints, etc.	External door opener	Induction loop	Tel. strobe	Possum	Bathroom controls	Total per room
Living room	1401					1000				100		1300		3901
Hall	1401	120	800						1100		40			3461
Kitchen	1401			75	150		2867		1100					5593
Bathroom	1401												1500	2901
													House total (ex VAT)	15,756

Figure 5.3: Estimated timescales for procurement and installation for subsequent projects

Edinvar Housing Association *Smart Homes* Timescale Estimates

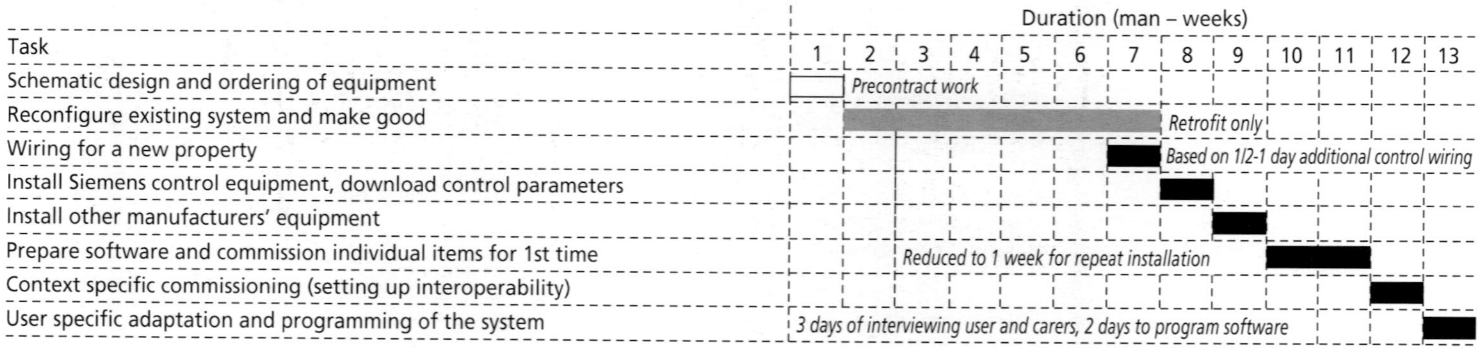

Joseph Rowntree Housing Association *Smart Homes* Timescale Estimates

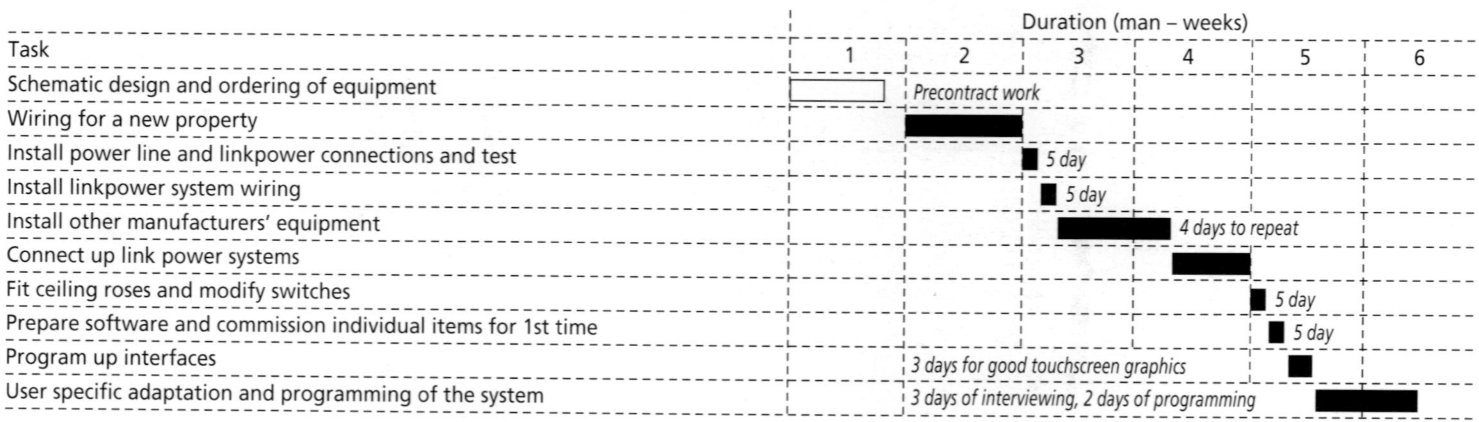

❑ 5.3 Operation: the views of visitors

The types of equipment and systems installed in the two demonstration houses are illustrated in Figures 5.4 and 5.5.

Figure 5.4: Equipment and facilities installed in York

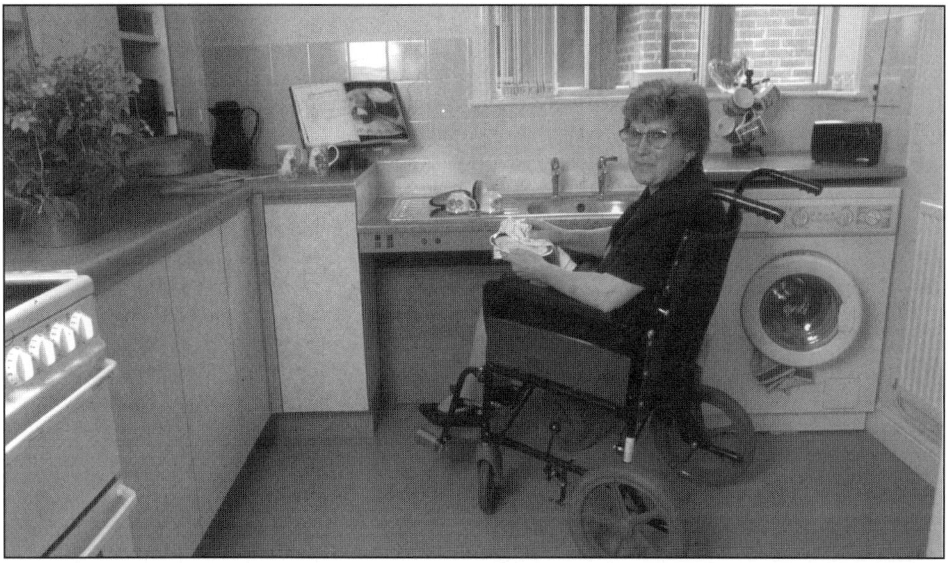

Sink in lowered position

Door entry camera and security control token

Figure 5.4: Equipment and facilities installed in York – contd.

PC-TV interface

Kitchen cupboard in lowered position

Figure 5.4: Equipment and facilities installed in York – contd.

Ceiling rose multi-function smoke detector head and infra-red detector

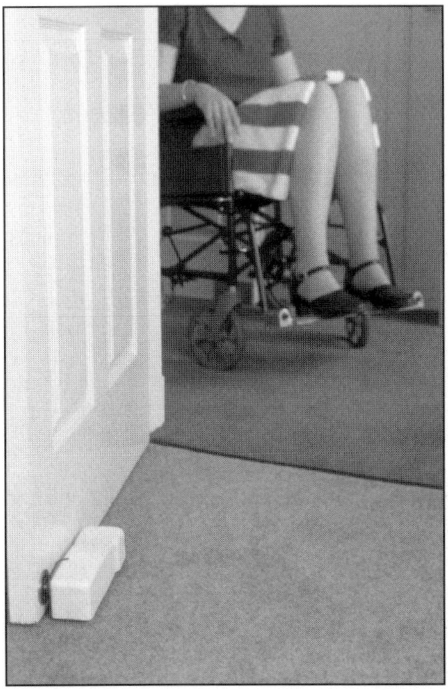

Door motor

Window motor

Figure 5.5: Equipment and facilities installed in Edinburgh

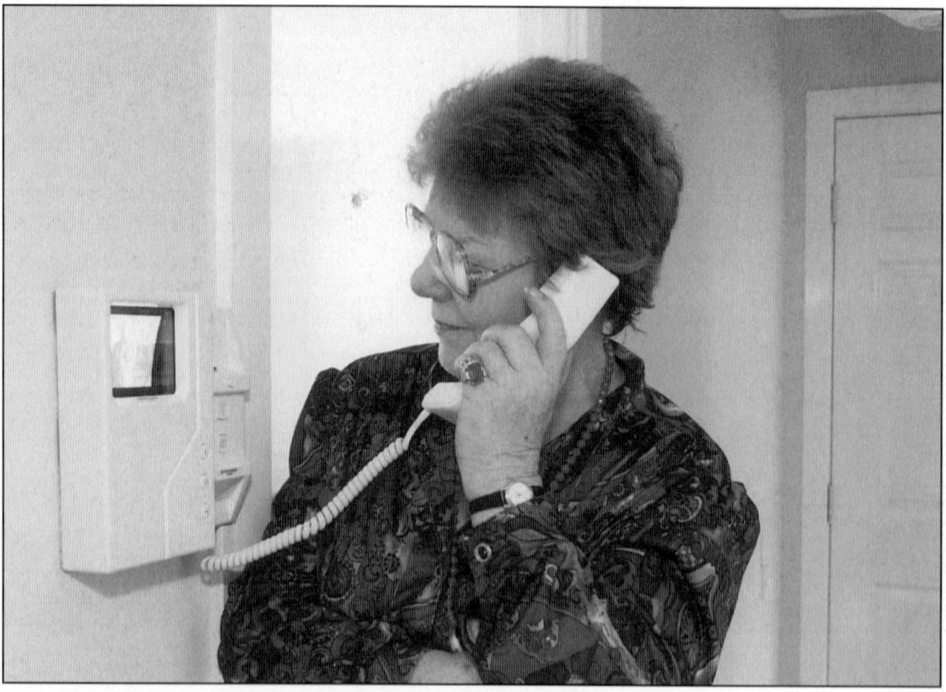

Door entry system

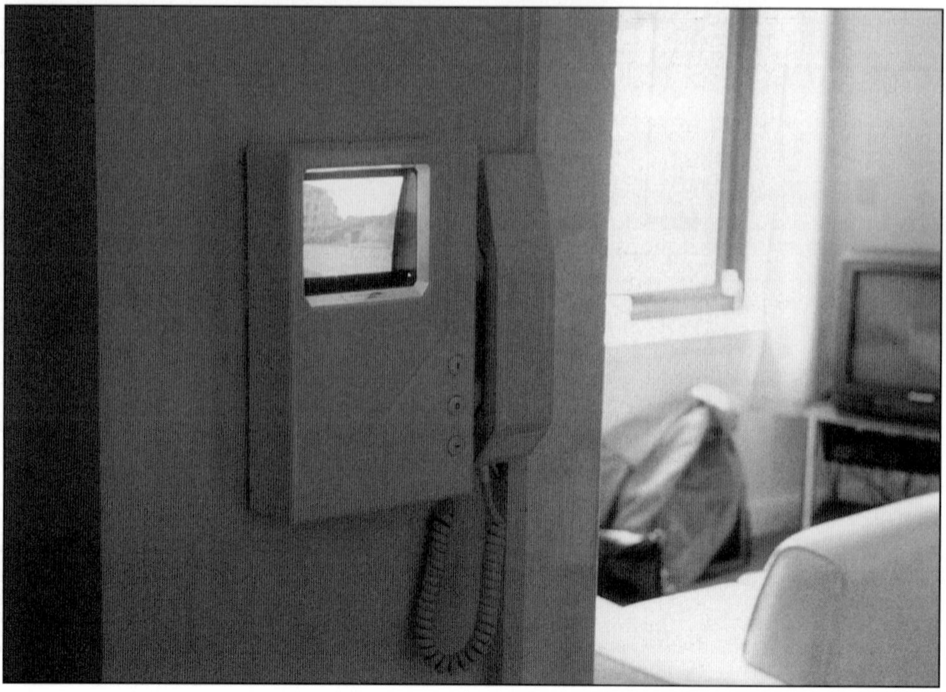

Figure 5.5: Equipment and facilities installed in Edinburgh – contd.

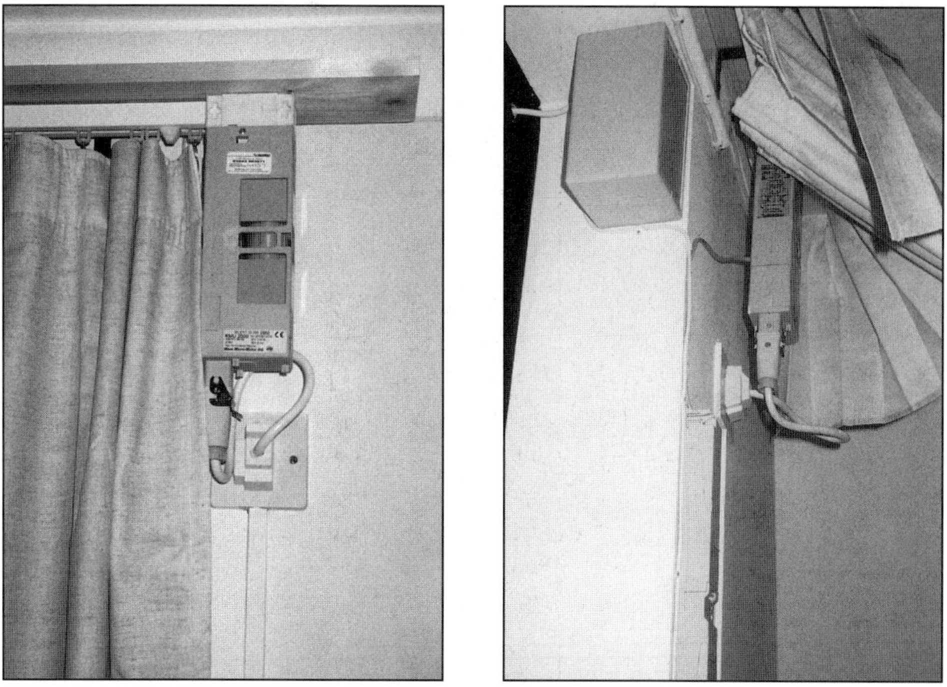

Curtain motors

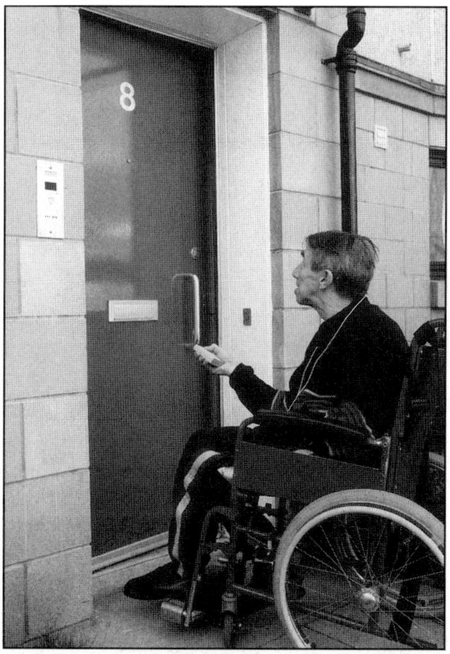

Remote control of front door

Figure 5.5: Equipment and facilities installed in Edinburgh – contd.

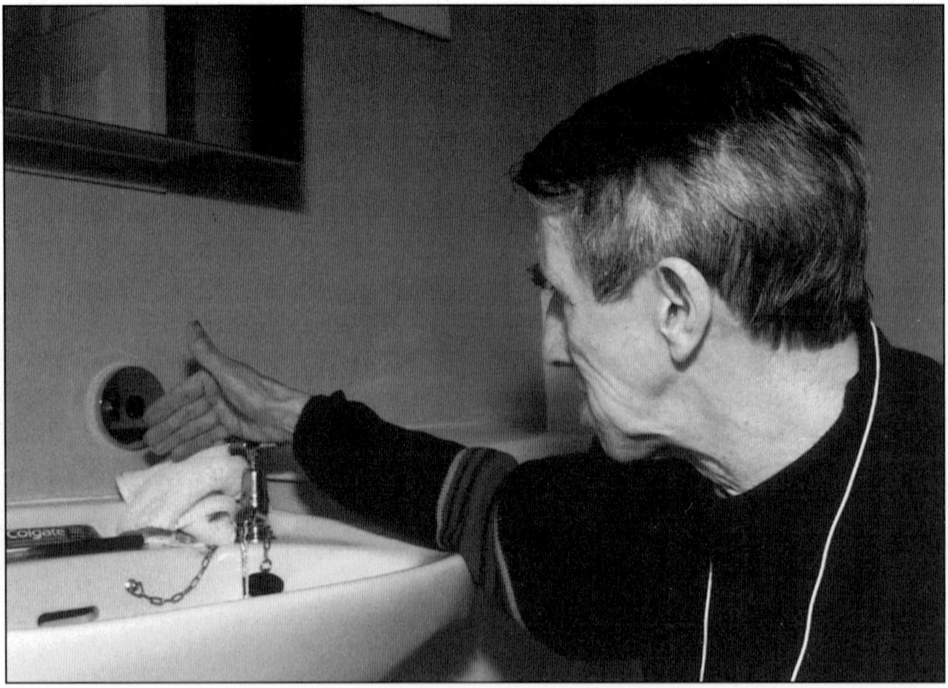

Movement sensitive tap controls

Figure 5.5: Equipment and facilities installed in Edinburgh – contd.

Light, curtain and power switches

At the time of writing, the demonstration homes had not been tested in full use with people living in them. One reason was the number of people interested in visiting the sites, which meant that they were kept open for six months longer than originally planned. Nevertheless, the project team were able to survey visitors' opinions using a questionnaire handed out at the sites. This provided valuable information about people's immediate reactions, likes and dislikes and viewpoints from a range of perspectives. It also provided an opportunity to compare views of the different approaches to *Smart Home* systems demonstrated in York and Edinburgh. A total of 88 responses were received, analysed below.

Table 5.4: Percentage of different types of people expressing an interest in the demonstration projects

Type of Person	Number (%)	Type of Person	Number (%)
Housing Provider	32	Tenant	6
Carer	17	N/R	5
Home Owner	14	Building contractor	4
Other	12	Equipment Supplier	2
Design	8		

Table 5.4 shows that there was a relatively even split of responses from those broadly classed as users and those that might be termed producers. It has been possible to compare some of the response sets from the questionnaire survey and identify any major differences between user and producer opinions. Table 5.5 shows that the majority of visitors were in the 26 to 60 year old age bands. Ideally, it would be useful to compare views and opinions between young and old people, but there were insufficient responses in these age bands to provide any meaningful analysis.

Table 5.5: Age distribution of respondents

Age	No. of visitors in age band (%)	Age	No. of visitors in age band (%)
<25	4	60+	6
26-40	30	N/R	9
40-60	51		

Respondents were asked to score a variety of different functions in terms of the importance they would attribute to them if it were possible to have such functions in their own homes. Based on a five point scale they scored one as being unimportant and five being important. Table 5.6 shows the ranking of importance based on the average responses from the questionnaires. This suggests that respondents considered issues of health, safety and security to be more important than comfort, control and labour saving devices.

Table 5.6: Importance attributed to different functions
(1 = unimportant, 5 = important)

Function	Importance	Function	Importance
Gas detection	4.7	Activity monitoring	4.0
Security alarm	4.6	Light switching controls	3.8
Warden call	4.6	Curtain opening device	3.7
Entry phone	4.4	Bathroom controls	3.7
Door opening device	4.3	Moveable kitchen units	3.7
Infra-red control	4.2	Light level control	3.5
Room heating controls	4.1	Touch screen display	3.2
Window opening device	4.0	Pressure pad switches	3.1

A similar approach was used to obtain views about the ease of use of different functions within the demonstration homes. The results are shown in Table 5.7, ranked from the most easy to use downwards. In terms of user interfaces for control of systems, there seems to be a preference for infra-red remote control units rather than the PC-based touch screen display. This could be a question of affordability (the PC and screen add considerably to the cost of installation) or purely an issue of familiarity with the hand held remote control equipment. In general, equipment and systems in the York demonstration home achieved a higher rating for ease of use than those in the Edinburgh project.

Table 5.7: Average ease of use scores, ranked by visitors
(1 = difficult, 5 = easy)

Function	Ease of use	Function	Ease of use
Gas detection	4.4	Curtain opening device	4.1
Pressure pad switches	4.3	Bathroom controls	4.1
Warden call	4.3	Infra-red control	4.1
Door opening device	4.2	Moveable kitchen units	4.1
Window opening device	4.2	Activity monitoring	4.0
Security alarm	4.2	Room heating controls	3.9
Entry phone	4.2	Light level control	3.9
Light switching controls	4.1	Touch screen display	3.6

Visitors to the demonstration homes were asked whether they would be prepared to pay more, either through rent or on the purchase price of their home, for *Smart Home* functions. It was recognised that providing *Smart Home* technologies would have a cost implication, and the vast majority of respondents were willing to pay more for added utility – Table 5.8. People generally expressed a willingness to pay between 5 and 10% more. This remains much lower than the actual costs of setting up the demonstration homes, although it is close to the projected costs if a volume market emerges and systems are produced using mass-produced components. It is unclear why all the respondents who were unwilling to pay more were visitors to the Edinburgh site.

Table 5.8: Amount of additional expenditure (either on purchase or through rent) respondents would pay for *Smart Home* systems

Additional amount prepared to spend	Number of respondents (%)
0%	6
5%	36
10%	29
15%	9
20%	3
No response	16

Respondents were asked to indicate between which sub-systems they would like to have interoperability. Visitors were asked to indicate this on a diagram illustrating the main systems within the dwelling. Table 5.9 illustrates the percentage of respondents choosing interoperability between different functional areas. Issues of safety and security dominate – a fire alarm system which can either activate or shut down other systems in the home is seen as especially important. Also significant is linking the security system to lighting, which would allow the mimicking of occupation when the security system is active and residents are away. Interoperability relating to comfort and labour saving functions seems to be of lesser importance.

Table 5.9: Importance of interoperability between different sub-systems and functional areas

Interoperability between sub-systems	No. of Respondents (%)
Fire/Security	71
Security/Lighting	55
Fire/Lighting	45
Fire/Heating	39
Fire/Appliances	39
Heating/Lighting	20
Entertainment/Appliances	18
Security/Heating	17
Entertainment/Lighting	16
Appliances/Lighting	16
Heating/Appliances	13
Heating/Entertainment	11
Security/Entertainment	10
Security/Appliances	9
Fire/Entertainment	5

Finally, one estate agent who visited the York *Smart Home* said that electronically controlled gates, doors and entry systems (including garage doors) were an enormous selling point, making properties potentially more attractive to future purchasers.

❑ 5.4 Technical assessment

It is not possible to provide a full and detailed assessment of technical performance and possible future applications in a trial limited to two demonstration sites. A far larger research and development programme would be required including extended tests with different user groups and many refinements to prototypes. Indeed, one of the difficulties in developing the *Smart Home* concept has been an inability on the part of housing producers to carry out the type of research, development, prototyping and testing that would be found in other industries producing sophisticated products. For example, new product development in the automobile industry often costs hundreds of millions of pounds and several hundred prototypes are built and tested in different environments before a new model is launched. In contrast, the *Smart Home* project was limited in scale and scope, costing no more than an estimated £250,000 in equipment, staff time and research. The following are therefore observations and comments about the technology and how it might be deployed, rather than rigorously proven research results.

■ Generic infrastructure

- *Echelon system:* it is unlikely that the LonWorks system will be suitable for retrofit or refurbishment applications in its bus wired form, using LonPoints as output and input nodes, because it requires installation of many individual devices. However, initial development work on the demonstrator board identified a number of ways in which the LonWorks system could be adapted for use in domestic retrofit, or refurbishment schemes. Echelon's licensing agreements with other manufacturers enabled design and production of customised multi-function components, reducing the number of visible parts and providing cost-effective solutions. Multi-function ceiling roses are an example of this, developed for the York project. This level of flexibility could also prove beneficial in new-build installations.

- *Siemens system:* the use of Bus systems – such as the Siemens EIBus in the Edinburgh project – requires considerable design and planning to ensure that it is routed around the building in the right place. However it provides a robust communications and control system with fail-safe modes providing back up in case of systems failure. Future developments of this system are planned to include EIB compatible powerline products, which could facilitate easier planning of cable layouts for both initial installation and subsequent adaptation.

Echelon and EIBus protocols were both originally designed to operate on cabled infrastructure, or bus systems. However, there have been considerable efforts on the part of manufacturers of both systems to develop installations that will also accommodate powerline signalling to devices. This could reduce the amount of work required to install and adapt systems in future.

- *Siemens and EIB equipment:* in general, the control equipment manufactured by Siemens and other EIB manufacturers is of excellent quality in terms of its engineering. However, it has been designed for use in commercial or industrial buildings and therefore appears to be over-engineered for normal use in the domestic environment. This has major cost implications, being too expensive to meet the 'affordability' criteria for normal use in housing. The equipment also has an industrial appearance, for example binary output fittings are very similar in appearance to fluorescent ballasts, which may well be ideal for fitting in strip luminaires but are awkward to conceal in a domestic setting – Figure 5.6.

- *Control and battery housings:* many of the items were delivered with large casings and cumbersome connections, which took up space and made installation time-consuming and expensive. Design of individual components, actuators, sensors and switches could be improved to enable discrete and rapid installation.

■ Terminal and subsidiary equipment

- *Door and window openers:* it was not possible to refine equipment or many of the systems demonstrated. One example is the large, cumbersome and noisy door and window opening devices. In future it will be technically feasible to develop doors and windows with these concealed in the

Figure 5.6: Siemens equipment – designed for use in commercial or industrial buildings

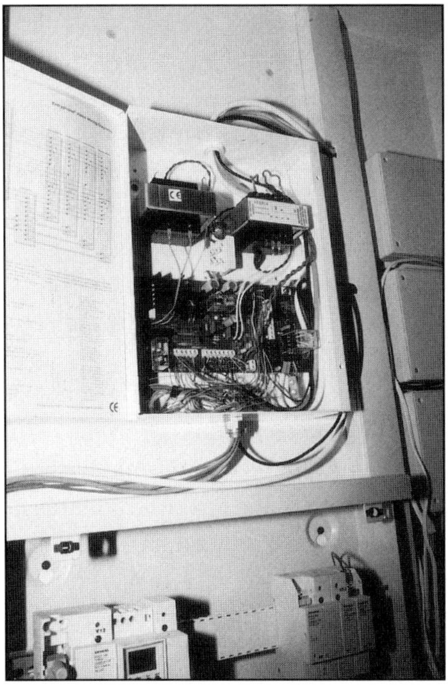

Various control boxes

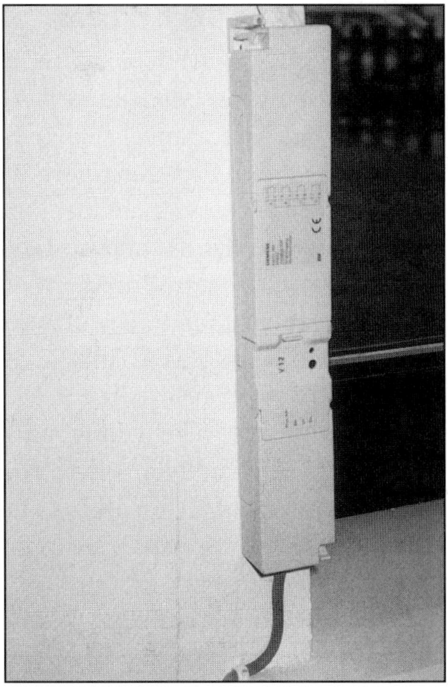

Binary output fitting

frames, in a similar way to electrically operated windows in car doors. However, it was not possible to develop these actuators on this project.

- *Non-EIB compatible components:* with the exception of Possum Controls, used to provide an interface for people with disabilities, it had not been possible to find other ancillary equipment with the facility to link to EIB networks for the Edinburgh project. This meant that additional control equipment had to be fitted, sometimes requiring internal modification of the equipment itself.

- *Other subsidiary equipment:* many items of terminal equipment lacked appropriate input and output modules to facilitate digital signalling and control. These had to be added to equipment or the network.

- *Equipment for special purposes:* many of the components and interfaces used to facilitate operation for people with disabilities has been designed for use in medical or 'institutional' environments. As such, it tends to be of an industrial appearance and over-engineered for use in domestic environments.

■ Rapid rate of change, adaptation in use and future development work

Many technologies were being improved and new systems developed during the period between 1996 and 1998, when the demonstration projects were built. The pace of technical change remains rapid, particularly in areas such as interoperability between discrete systems and component parts, and in the provision of new services in the home. *Smart Home* systems can therefore be described as 'immature' and unstable. It is likely that new vintages of technology will be introduced within a relatively short period – say 3 to 5 years. Current installations will need to be designed with change in mind so that they can be upgraded at little extra cost.

Users are unlikely to be willing to invest in technologies that may rapidly become obsolete and will want assurance that they will be compatible with new generations of terminal equipment and devices, as well as upgradeable when new generations of infrastructural systems are introduced. Such requirements will put extra burdens on manufacturers and systems integrators adding to existing pressures to improve their performance. For example, there is room for major improvements on the part of equipment and component manufacturers in the design and supply of parts, components and systems, as well as in providing appropriate product support services. Design for integration and installation appears to have been overlooked, in the belief that technologies proven in the commercial office environment can be easily down-sized and adapted for use in the home. This proved not to be the case.

Moreover, there is generally poor understanding of the design of technologies for use in the home. Manufacturers and suppliers lack appropriate services in terms of systems capabilities to assist in integration, installation and commissioning. Given the current level of development of these technologies it is doubtful whether manufacturers and the supply industries have the capability to deliver without expert procurement knowledge on the part of the client. It is therefore essential that the integration process is properly organised with single point responsibility and appropriate skills for design and installation.

CHAPTER 6

DIGITAL FUTURES

Once you break the bounds of your bag of skin … you will also begin to blend into the architecture. In other words, some of your electronic organs may be built into the surroundings. … 'inhabitation' will take on a new meaning – one that has less to do with parking your bones in architecturally defined space and more with connecting your nervous system to nearby electronic organs. Your room and your home will become part of you and you will become part of them.
(Mitchell 1995: 30)

This somewhat disturbing vision of the future may not be as far fetched as it first appears. The image conjured in Mitchell's quote may seem terrifying to some, yet scientifically and technically, society is on the verge of developing interfaces which will allow people to manipulate new digital systems from within and outside their homes. The development of bio-informatic technologies will potentially facilitate far greater control without the need to use cumbersome physical interfaces such as the QWERTY keyboard.

The two demonstration sites illustrate the possibilities for automation and communication in the home. At present, most of the British housing stock is not equipped with the cabling, switching or two-way transmission devices needed for interactivity – they are limited in use to one-way broadcasting applications. As many more homes in Britain connect to the Internet and with the potential of digital TV, more people are likely to demand a new infrastructure to allow them to connect to interactive digital services.

Panasonic, a major consumer electronics manufacturer, has a particular vision of the future for consumer information appliances, including a number of systems to provide 'information for living' – Table 6.1. Other Japanese consumer-electronics manufacturers continue to add new functions to existing products. For example, NEC has designed a micro-wave cooker with a flat screen display located in the door. Matsushita Electric is experimenting with prototype robot pets for elderly people. The aim is to develop cuddly toys for adults which can transmit data about their owners' well-being to support services.

Is there a precedent for such changes in the home? Examples of electrification and provision of central heating in homes illustrate new levels of comfort, safety, cleanliness and a generally higher quality of life. There are also analogies with people's fears of unknown aspects of these technologies: for example, concern that electricity would leak from sockets is perhaps similar to current concerns about information 'leaking' from computer networks. Today's drivers for change are also similar to those of the past – to improve the domestic living environment – but they also include the need to support many new functions, including the use of interactive services and ability for older people to maintain independent lifestyles in their own homes. Once potential benefits of integrated *Smart Home* systems have been proven it is likely that more people will be prepared to purchase them – in a similar way to investment in electricity or central heating in the home earlier this century. Systems will only then begin to diffuse throughout the housing stock, costs will fall and a new supply industry will emerge.

Yet this research project has shown that in Britain, *Smart Home* markets, technologies and supply industries are immature. Consumers are ignorant or sceptical about potential benefits; technologies are difficult to integrate for interoperability; the industry is fragmented and there are no one-stop-shop suppliers providing a full range of bundled products and services.

In spite of the problems encountered in integrating systems in the demonstration projects, technical issues of this nature are probably the easiest to resolve. Within a few years, technical questions about whether to use separately cabled bus systems or power line carriers to form basic infrastructures are likely to have been answered. The main requirements will be to provide housing with simple, robust, basic infrastructures to support many types of increasingly portable equipment. Robustness, reliability and ease of installation are likely to be the key determinants for success in generic infrastructure systems. People are unlikely to be willing to invest in such technologies if there is a legacy of systems failures and software bugs.

Technologies which simplify, routinise and automate functions in commercial buildings may not be so desirable in the home where people generally wish

Table 6.1: Panasonic's vision of the future for consumer information appliances

Technology	Service
Large flat-screen displays	Serving as multi-media interactive windows on the digital world, located in the living room for use with digital broadcasting and the Internet.
Home server	A computer storing digital pictures recorded on home video, or directly from TV programmes.
On-line information services	Systems to arrange for home-delivery of food and other provisions, including automatic data transfer of cooking instructions to the networked microwave and cooker.
Networked fridge	A fridge with 'stock control' functions providing information about the food in stock at home, including use-by dates. Information can be accessed remotely to assess what is in stock, if out shopping.
Remote control	Remote display of information relating to consumption in the home, including use of gas, water and electricity.
On-line health check system	Sensors and a camera which measures and checks body temperature, blood pressure, electro-cardiogram and blood sugar. Data is stored in the home computer and can be sent on a daily basis to the hospital or health clinic, facilitating medical consultation and services while at home.
Health toilet system	A toilet which measures and checks weight, body fat and urine samples. Data is stored in the home computer and can be sent to medical professionals.
Computer for work	A home-working computer, linked to the Internet.
On-line machine maintenance services	Services which provide advice following self-diagnostics about the status and operating functions of digital appliances in the home. Defects and failures are automatically reported immediately to the maintenance company.
Energy control system	An internal environmental control system linked to ventilation, lighting, air-conditioning and heating systems, to provide optimised environmental comfort whilst minimising energy use.

Source: Panasonic brochure, translated by Ritsuko Ozaki, SPRU.

to remain free from technical constraints. Understanding and organising social issues related to the new digital future in the home are likely to present a far more difficult problem than resolving technical matters. This research project was unable to do more than indicate the need for studies of the effects on privacy, ownership and control, finance, exclusion and inclusion and the ethics of use. Far larger trials will be needed to understand these.

It seems certain, however, that the design and spatial layout of houses will need to change to accommodate life in the digital future. For example, the TV was instrumental in introducing a new pattern of domestic life, with people typically spending a number of hours each day in front of the set (Jonscher 1999: 215). This did not create a new 'fixed' pattern of life at home, because the advent of video recorders meant that people could choose the timing of their viewing habits, introducing new forms and more flexibility to living patterns.

Technological change and new activities in the home have therefore transformed its layout and provision of equipment over the past century. Analogies can be made between the provision of a single socket outlet in many homes in the early days of electrification, and the single telephone point in many of today's new houses. As Mitchell (1995: 172) argues, building the new programmable places will not just be a matter of pulling wires through gaps in walls and connecting electronic boxes in different rooms. New displays and interfaces will be invented and these may replace parts of the traditional fabric and facades of buildings. Architects and designers will have to confront new choices between providing for physical activities and the new virtual spaces. It may soon be necessary for houses to be designed with special deposit boxes to receive home deliveries of shopping ordered over the Internet when occupiers are away.

❑ 6.1 Creating markets for *Smart Homes*

Who should do what in order to promote user-centred development and implementation of *Smart Home* systems? Many people are involved in building new homes and refurbishing the existing stock, including: owners, occupiers, designers and engineers, developers and social landlords, contractors and technology suppliers, installers, planners and regulators, financiers and insurers. In housing for frail older people or those with disabilities, social services and healthcare professionals are also likely to be involved. It is therefore likely to take time before all the necessary organisations have understood the implications for their own methods of working and become familiar with the potential benefits and constraints to implementing *Smart Home* systems.

User inputs are of critical importance in creating the market for *Smart Homes.* Expert advice will be needed to help users understand what is possible. But specifications must be derived from functional needs identified by users, not only from technological possibilities, if consumer confidence is to grow.

What financial arrangements can be developed to help pay for the costs of *Smart Home* systems? Can they be built into service charges for buildings or estates? Will equipment be provided and installed free by providers charging for the use of new interactive services? How will the installation of systems affect the value of housing? These are important issues, particularly in the affordable housing marketplace, but they are only likely to be resolved over time through the development of more extensive trials and demonstration projects.

What role do standards play in helping to create a market? In spite of the slow pace in agreeing common standards, technical development has been rapid with convergence occurring between systems as manufacturers struggle to understand their potential roles in emerging markets. Most European manufacturers have tended to focus on:

- simple on-off switching systems for selected applications, requiring no additional network installation (e.g. remote control switching);
- discrete systems for selected applications but with wider functional scope, requiring specific network installation (e.g. security and heating control systems).

There are no suppliers providing fully integrated systems and services. To motivate consumers to buy their products, suppliers will therefore need to fill this gap, providing products and services that operate as:

- *generic technologies*, the basic, standard compatible building blocks, supporting;
- *context-specific systems*, adaptable to a wide variety of dwelling types, facilitating;
- *personalised systems*, tailored to specific individual and household requirements.

Table 6.2 illustrates the types of activity required to establish a market. At present the primary customer state for integrated *Smart Home* systems could be described as one of 'unconscious inactivity'. However, many of the discrete sub-systems have already progressed to stage 4. Experience in the York and Edinburgh demonstration projects would suggest that the key issue in developing consumer confidence for more widespread market growth will be the ability to provide services to support the use of new products and systems.

Networking different devices within the home often involves the installation of considerable amounts of cabling to carry signals for data, voice and video. While this is relatively straightforward when the dwelling is being built, retrofitting existing dwellings is far more expensive and disruptive, as was experienced in the demonstration projects. Nevertheless, Britain builds comparatively few new homes each year and this may prompt more manufacturers to seek ways of retrofitting existing housing: for example using existing power lines, radio frequency or infrared media for communicating signals – Figure 6.1.

Table 6.2: Market development model

	Primary customer state	Market state	Typical activity required
Stage 1	Unconscious inactivity	No market	Product development, market research, education, standards
Stage 2	Conscious inactivity	Emerging market	Demonstrations, measurement of benefits, dissemination, supply chain development, education, training
Stage 3	Conscious activity	Growth market	Quality control, market support, training
Stage 4	Unconscious activity	Established market	Consolidation, refinement, monitoring, challenge conventional wisdom

Source: from a chart drawn by Alan Kell, European Intelligent Building Group.

Figure 6.1: Market potential and technical solutions

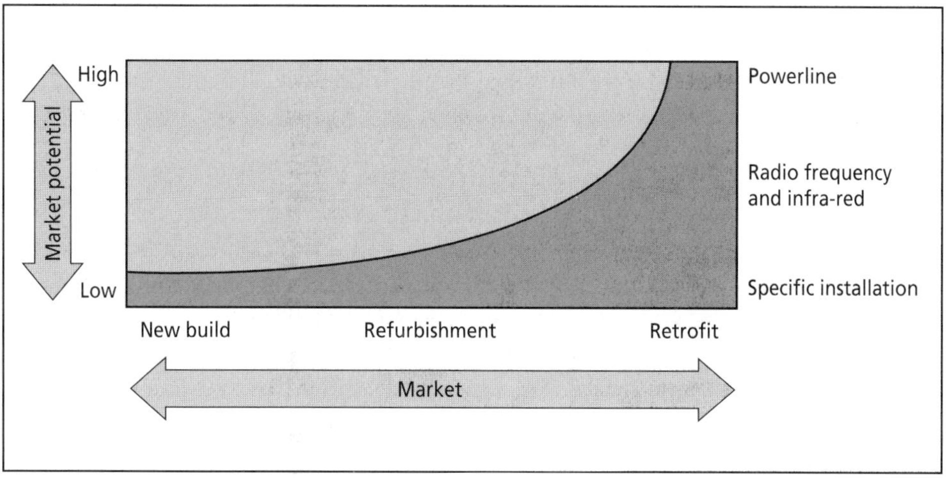

Source: developed from Jeck (1997).

Not only have suppliers failed to convey the benefits of *Smart Home* systems to individual consumers, housing providers and landlords have a restricted perception of what the concept can offer. The main housing developers and contractors are largely unaware of the potential benefits of *Smart Home* technologies and therefore do not take a lead in introducing the concept to purchasers. A common view amongst housing associations specialising in housing for older people – an area where there have been some efforts to develop *Smart Home* applications – saw the technology providing only marginal benefits (Gann et al 1995). There are a few notable exceptions to these views, including developers such as Wilcon – involved in producing the INTEGER house – and smaller builders of luxury schemes, such as Rice Homes. An increasing number of housing associations are also beginning to express an interest in these technologies particularly with around 4,000 dwellings for older people built annually. This could form the basis of a new market.

❑ 6.2 Technology suppliers and integrators

Manufacturers and suppliers face three challenges if they are to develop a market for their products:

- improve their understanding of user needs;
- improve the organisation of supply distribution channels;
- develop generic products and service suitable for a wide range of housing types.

A significant problem for suppliers is the need to convey to potential users a set of perceived benefits, and deliver bundled products and services so that these benefits can be realised. For customers, only a comprehensive package of benefits is likely to make-up for large-scale initial investment – customer value-added is the *benefit* of the system, not its 'smartness' or 'intelligence'.

Developing more consumer oriented distribution channels via retailers (as has happened with the X-10 products in the USA) *may* stimulate greater interest in the medium term. However, while some basic equipment could be sold via existing channels such as kitchen planners or consumer electronics retailers, more complex applications require specialist integration and installation within wider networks. Systems integrators are needed who can bridge the gaps between each of the traditional players in housing markets, offering advice on applications, the individual configuration of systems, installation and after-sales service.

Installers, retailers and manufacturers are likely to face growing competition from multiple service providers. These are companies which aspire to deliver shopping, entertainment, banking and other interactive services direct to consumers – Figure 6.2. Energy suppliers, for example, are becoming multi-utility providers. Driven partly by a search for new business because of competition in their traditional activities, these companies are diversifying into value-added services such as energy consulting, automated invoicing, telecoms and facilities management. During the next decade, new 'information utilities' companies may emerge, selling services to residents in their homes (Birnbaum 1999).

Figure 6.2: Competition in the emergent *Smart Home* market

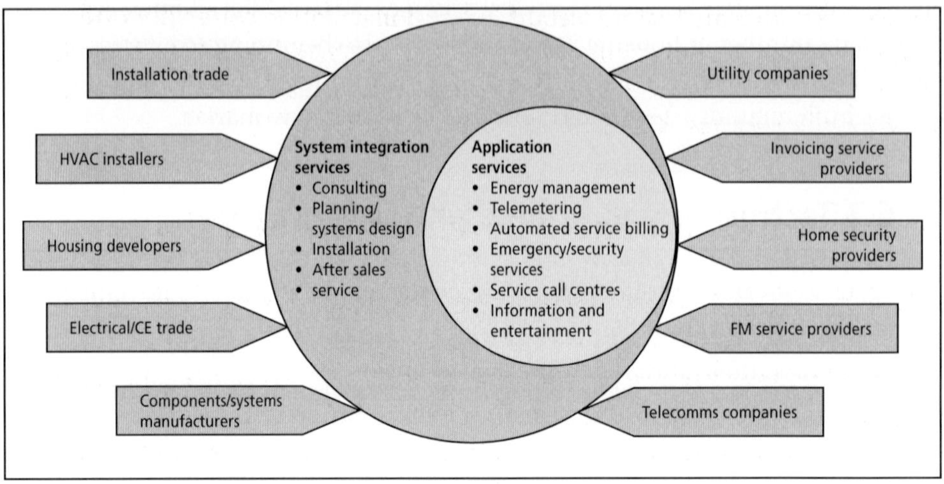

Source: derived from Jeck (1997).

❑ 6.3 Training issues

The first lesson from the demonstration projects was the need to obtain new in-house technical expertise to design, procure and integrate systems, in order to proceed. In the current phase of technical development and market penetration, it is difficult to conceive how an organisation wishing to develop *Smart Homes* could do so, without investing heavily in training and internal technical capabilities.

Physical installation work is likely to be within the current capabilities of qualified electricians: the fitting of components by electricians was monitored on one of the demonstration projects. Programming and commissioning are more complex activities but with training in computer skills, they should also be within the scope of a qualified electrician. Training for use of specific software is likely to be necessary. Once the system is installed updating programmes is a relatively simple job for someone trained on the software.

In addition to these skills it would useful for training to include an understanding of:

- devices which operate using new forms of communication and user interfaces;
- interconnectivity between different sub-systems and equipment;
- management and co-ordination of different suppliers in provision of new systems;
- the need to be aware of future technical developments.

However, it appears that housebuilders and installation contractors are training too few people to meet demand in their current markets let alone meet the needs of installing *Smart Home* systems should the market grow rapidly in future (see: Construction Industry Board 1998).

❑ 6.4 Future research and development activities

The breadth and diversity of the potential user community, the variable context in which products and services are used, and the need for manufacturers to balance usability and other design goals make the reality of user-centred design complex. Moreover, it would have proven virtually impossible to investigate people's potential requirements for products and services without the development of demonstration projects.

Yet it appears that many of the emerging products and systems are being developed with only limited understanding of user needs and little user participation. Future research based on trials with real users in real situations will be essential. This could include time and motion studies with different user groups to explore where benefits are gained and obstacles are experienced. Little things matter. For example, the speed at which interfaces respond, or the positioning of control points. It is unlikely that usability issues, defects, quality and fail-safe capabilities will be resolved without an iterative approach involving feed back from successive generations of prototypes.

Many questions about use of *Smart Home* systems remain unanswered. For example, people may have reservations about increased automation, but they may also want the benefits, yet they need to be sure that they have overriding control. Control and access to control through appropriate interfaces may well form the basis of new disputes in the home. One resident commented that it is bad enough arguing over whether to watch Coronation Street or the Football on TV, let alone competing for access to the Web or Home Management system. In another example, questions were raised about potential changes to the dynamics of relationships between people in the home. For instance, who has access to, and knowledge about, the technology when carers and visitors enter the home? Understanding complex issues associated with ethics, privacy, inclusion and exclusion will require detailed observational work.

Further research is also required on attitudes towards managing energy and the internal environment. The use of *Smart Home* technologies is beginning to be linked to issues of sustainable development (for example, the Intelligent and Green – INTEGER project), yet there was no real sense of importance attributed to environmental concerns in the York and Edinburgh demonstration projects. Better information about methods of monitoring energy usage and advising users on consequences of their decisions should be welcomed, particularly in the social housing sector. It should, however, be noted that carers from the demonstration projects expressed some concern that less well-off people might be dissuaded from using central heating if, for example, 'real-time' monitoring of expenditure on energy were available. The implication being that they would try to conserve even more of their scarce resources and may suffer from the cold.

Development work is continuing at both the York and Edinburgh sites. At York, *Smart Home* systems are to be installed in the home of a young man, paralysed from the waist down. The resident uses a wheelchair in his home, which he shares with his able-bodied partner, with only minor adaptations. It is hoped that the addition of a number of *Smart Home* systems will provide considerable benefits. The systems will be monitored to evaluate ease of use and training implications. Servicing and maintenance will also be assessed. Lessons from this site will be incorporated into three installations planned for the Park Lodge development at New Earswick.

In addition to long-term testing, Joseph Rowntree Housing Trust intend to continue with their collaborative work with equipment suppliers in refining *Smart Home* products. Particular attention will be paid to aesthetic design to enable products to fit unobtrusively within most domestic environments. Work will also continue to ensure that products have appropriate levels of intelligence for their applications.

In Edinburgh, further technical development work is planned. This will involve health and activity *monitoring* with residents, in collaboration with Tunstall Telecom, including remote monitoring and signalling. This work will connect the on-site Resource Centre with the demonstration flat either via land-line (cable) or telephone link (modem). It will involve building further interfaces between Siemens control equipment, video entryphone systems and Tunstall's equipment. Touchscreen technology will also be tested in use as a simple pictorial interface for the control of domestic equipment (e.g. telephone dialling, window, door and curtain operation). It may also be tested as a memory aid for people with mild forms of dementia.

Appendix 1

Technical Specifications

■ York

- The house consists of 63 nodes (Devices) that operate on 2 channels (The Network).
  - Channel 1 is the Link power (Combined 48V & Data) and FTT (Free Topology Transceiver which is Data). On this channel there are 41 nodes including: window openers, door openers, cupboard lifters, tap controls, smoke detectors, passive infra-red detectors, infra-red receivers, video switches, door entry and Lonpoints.
  - Channel 2 is Power line, on this channel there are 21 nodes, including: ceiling roses, plug controllers, fan controllers and fluorescent lights.
- The 2 channels are bound together with the Power supply.
- The Power supply node is a battery-backed supply for the Link power & FTT.
- It also has a Power line router which allows Data to pass between the two channels.
- The programming is done with a package called Lonmaker™ for Windows™.
- Most nodes work on a clock rate of between 5 and 10Mhz, or at powers of 2 x 625Khz.

Basic functions

Control Equipment – All non 240V equipment has been pre-wired with 'bus' wiring to accept data signalling. Sensors and actuators associated with heating control and security have been fitted.

Window Motors – Installed and fully operational. Units can be operated via an infra-red (IR) remote control.

Curtain Motors – Installed and fully operational. A light sensor is fitted to the site to allow automatic control at dusk/dawn.

Door Motors – Installed and fully operational. Control is via IR with a manual switch adjacent to the door. Doors can still be opened by hand with pressure equivalent to a hydraulic door closer.

Video Entry System – Installed and fully operational.

Keyless Door System – Installed and operational, the 'Dallas token' used to operate this system also activates or disables the security alarm.

Bathroom Controls – IR pads have been fitted to control wash hand-basin taps, bath taps and toilet flush. Flow of water is time-limited.

Kitchen Equipment – Cupboard and sink lifting equipment is fitted and taps have had electronic valves fitted. All of these are controlled by switches mounted at worktop height.

See Figure A1.1.

■ Edinburgh

- The home network consists of approximately 55 nodes (Bus-Coupling Units, Binary Inputs/Outputs etc) that are connected to a 2-wire bus system (The Network), and provide interconnection to all of the devices controlled within the dwelling, either directly (for those that are EIB compatible), or via the devices' own interfaces (usually relay-based). The 2-wire cable carries both data and power. Power (28 Volts DC) can be used by any actuators or controls connected to the bus, if they do not use external power supplies (e.g. lighting relays, motorised radiator valves). Binary data is carried in the form of an AC signal carrier. To prevent this AC signal affecting the DC power supply, a Choke is fitted to the PSU.
- All of the data transmission between nodes and devices occurs on the bus, other than those signals that originate from infra-red devices (remote controls, disabled persons interfaces). Even then, infra-red data is translated into bus-compatible signals via an IR interface.
- Programming and commissioning the system is achieved by the use of ETS (EIB Tools Software), which is a Windows-based environment.
- The Touch screen Interface is connected to the bus system and its associated devices using bridging/visualisation software – CnC 'Unihub'. Unihub is broadly based on the 'Visual Basic' software package.

A1.1: Schematic design for the York Smart Home

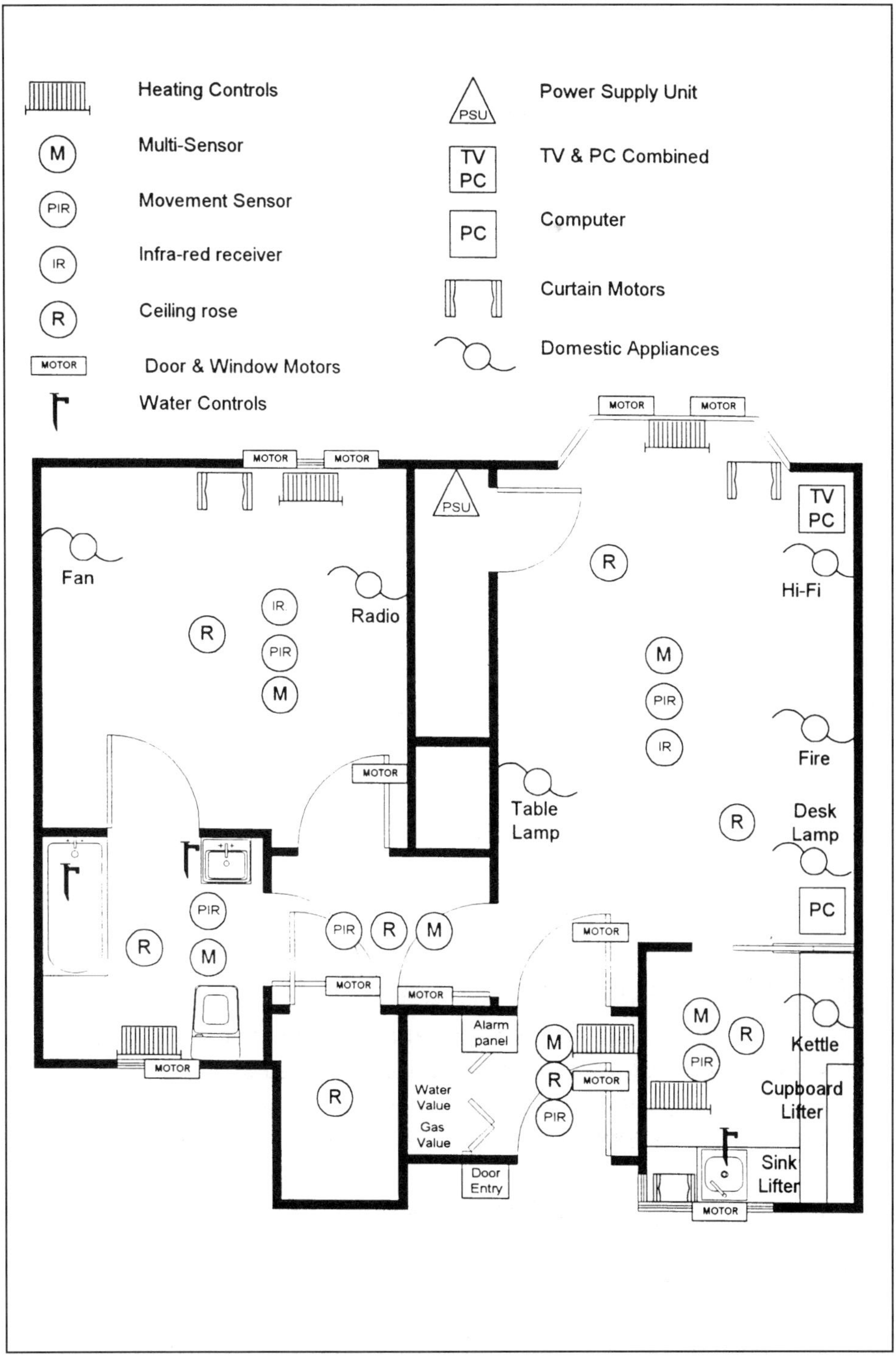

Basic functions

Control Equipment (Siemens) – The system is dispersed throughout the house, but some devices are located in a cupboard in the kitchen. These include: power supply for communication (bus) system; lighting relays, shutter (window) switches; timers; logic modules; video entryphone control box; alarm 'radio' triggers; power failure backup (when fitted).

All rooms have been pre-wired with 'bus' wiring to accept Siemens devices. Sensors and actuators associated with heating control and security have been fitted but are awaiting commissioning.

Window Motors – All windows with the exception of the bathroom are fitted with motors to open and close them. They can be operated using IR remote controls including the disabled persons interface, and by using a set of wall switches. Interaction with other equipment is possible including the heating and security systems. Window sensors allow the dwelling to know at any time whether windows are open or closed.

Curtain Motors – Curtains have motor driven tracks fitted and can be operated using the same range of devices as described with the window controls. There is also an external light sensor that allows the curtains to be opened and closed automatically. The curtains can also be linked with operations of other equipment (e.g. lighting).

Door Motors – Fitted to front and back doors. These can work in either fully automatic mode, or in 'Power Assist' mode, where the user is aided in opening the door. The doors can also be opened in the conventional manner, offering no more weight to the door than a conventional hydraulic door closer. The system is currently set up so that doors can be unlocked and opened in conjunction with a remote control (including a disabled person's interface or touchscreen), an externally mounted sensor and 'swipe' key, a wall mounted push-pad, or via the entryphone system. The system can also be configured so that doors can be unlocked in an emergency (e.g. in the event of a fire). Contacts fitted to the doors allow the dwelling to know if the property is unsecured or if a user has fallen in an open doorway.

Video Entry System – A video-telephone is fitted in the hall, and the video images are also relayed to the TV in the living-room. The user can switch to the video image on the TV and then speak to the caller via an audio link through the Scart socket on the TV. The image could be relayed to another room (e.g. bedroom) or off-site to a warden or carer.

A1.2: Schematic design for the Edinburgh Smart Home

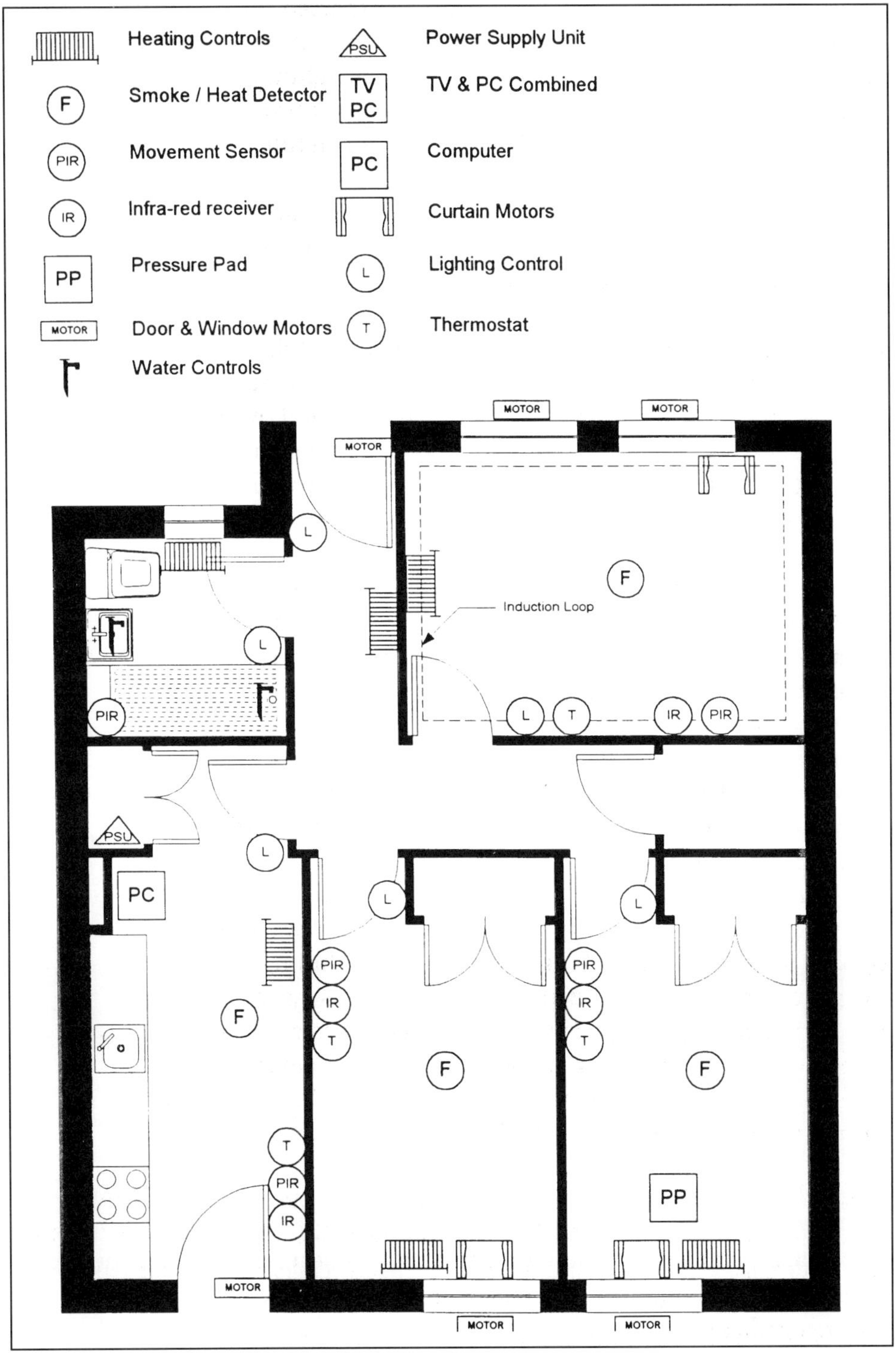

Keyless Door System – Sensors are fitted to the door posts of the front and the back doors, and these are used to unlock and open the doors without the use of a traditional key. The sensor is activated using a 'swipe' unit about the size of a keyring fob. Extra swipes can be programmed as necessary and lost or stolen swipes can be deleted from the system.

Lighting Controls – Lighting can controlled from standard wall switches or from IR remote controls, or automatically (e.g. by software timer or light sensor). Lighting circuits are wired independently rather than in the more traditional 'ring' format. No dimming actuators have been fitted, but the current installation would make modification a simple option.

Bathroom Controls – The bathroom has been fitted with a 'level entry' shower cubicle. This allows wheelchair or walking-frame users to take a shower with little or no assistance. A half-height shower screen means that carers can assist in bathing without getting wet.

The wash hand-basin and the shower both have infra-red ('no touch') controls fitted, which allow those with poor manual dexterity to operate taps and shower. The timing of the water flow can be altered, and the hot water supply can be thermostatically regulated.

The toilet is a combined bidet ('Shower Toilet') and WC. The toilet can wash and blow dry users, with little or no help from the carer. The toilet is awaiting the fitting of an interface to allow the flush to be activated using an infra-red sensor.

Heating Controls – Radiators have motorised valves, and every room (except the bathroom) has a wall-mounted thermostat. Heating can be 'zoned' so that individual control of temperature is available in every room, or one control can be used to regulate the whole house. For those people unable to operate wall-mounted thermostats, an IR remote control or the disabled person's interface can be programmed to perform that function. Integration of the system components means that the heating can link into other devices including ensuring that windows are closed when the heating comes on. The room thermostats are also capable of monitoring temperature levels and detecting potential risk situations such as temperatures dropping to unsafe levels. This information can be relayed to the warden via the 'Community' Alarm telephone.

'Community' Alarm Telephone and other Safety Devices – The telephone base unit allows calls to be made to a Call-Centre in the event of an accident or other emergency. The Call Centre is operated by Hanover Housing Association. A pendant unit, if activated by the user, will make an emergency call, but the system is also linked to three alarm 'triggers' that require no direct action by the user. One trigger is linked to a low temperature alarm, another to smoke, gas and heat alarms, and the third to movement detectors, pressure pads, and devices that would indicate inactivity. The heat/smoke/gas alarms when activated would make emergency calls to the carer. The cooker alarm is also linked to a safety device that will automatically cut off the supply (gas or electricity) to the stove. Even after the alarms have stopped, the supply can only be reinstated by using a reset key (usually kept by the carer). The activity alarm is linked to movement detectors (PIRs) fitted in every room, pressure pads fitted at the sides of the bed, and also located in other areas of the dwelling. Any uncharacteristic lulls in activity or if the user has not been registered as having got out of bed means that a call can be made to care staff automatically. Other equipment functions can also be used to raise an inactivity alarm, and these include: operation of lights; opening doors/windows, opening curtains; toilet flush or operation of shower/wash hand-basin.

Loop Induction Amplifier – Fitted in the living-room. This allows hearing aid users to hear the TV, radio, or the doorbell, without these devices being uncomfortably loud for people with good hearing. There is also a strobe 'repeater' lamp fitted that flashes when the telephone rings – again, for the hard of hearing.

Audible Reminders – Voice modules that record and store speech digitally have been tried to assess their value. Potential use is with memory facilities for example to remind users to close windows and lock doors, or to remind people to take medication.

'Touchscreen' Interface – A touchscreen provides users with a pictorial remote control. It has been considered as useful for those with learning difficulties and/or cognitive impairment. The touchscreen interfaces with the dwelling's control system and allows the user to operate devices by touching an image on the screen (e.g. opening the door). The touchscreen requires a computer enabling other functions to be harnessed with the touchscreen including spoken prompts and recorded video images.

Burglar Alarm and Other Miscellaneous Devices – The burglar alarm has the potential to be linked to the control system in the house. At the present time, the burglar alarm can utilise the sensors that the dwelling is already using for other functions (e.g. pressure pads, window/door contacts, movement detectors).

An Uninterruptible Power Supply (UPS) will be fitted to ensure continuity of operation of equipment in the event of a mains failure. Devices connected will include door mechanisms and door locks, and where appropriate, the PC/touchscreen interface.

There are two IR receivers fitted in the dwelling. These are situated in the living-room and the main bedroom. This allows the designated IR remote controls interface to be used in the bedroom.

See Figure A1.2.

■ Installation experiences

Rowntree

In order to have a more cost effective installation and to have devices more suited to a domestic environment some bespoke equipment had to be commissioned. Cabling has not proved to be a major issue with only around 100 metres of additional cabling required in the bungalow.

Edinvar

Delays – The late arrival of Siemens equipment and delays with the Siemens training course have caused difficulties. Undoubtedly there has been a serious underestimation of the amount of work involved in the cabling and installation work. As an indicator of this, by the time all installation is finished, there is likely to be an additional 350-400 metres of extra cable installed in the flat.

Wiring – To allow room by room control of lighting circuits via the Siemens equipment, all lighting circuits in the flat – 9 in total – had to be rewired. This was both time-consuming and messy, and has led to a need for complete redecoration of the demonstrator site. With the addition of circuits for other equipment, the electrical distribution board is approaching its maximum capacity.

Modifications to Building Structure/Fixtures – To accommodate some equipment or to make it operate correctly, major and minor changes have been made. These include the relocation of the doors within their frames to allow door motors to operate smoothly, modification of window locks to fit motor controls, stripping out the bathroom, removal of skirting boards and refixing them using cup washers and screws etc. Whilst the existing 'homebus' voids behind skirting boards have been used, siting of radiators and other fixtures has made the fitting of cable trunking necessary. If some or all of the technologies used are to be replicated elsewhere, changes to existing building specifications will need to be considered.

APPENDIX 2

TECHNICAL STANDARDS

By Ken Bromley, BRE

1 Introduction

This report reviews communications protocols with the potential for application in *Smart Homes* and residential buildings, including in links to remote control centres. Applications include management and control of heating, ventilation and air conditioning (HVAC), lighting control, fire detection and prevention, security and access control (including the use of video), metering of fuel and power, telemedicine, etc.

All the protocols described below have to a greater or lesser extent become accepted standards, having gained the support either of an association of manufacturers or of European and international standardisation committees.

1.1 Communications levels

Communications networks can be conveniently grouped into four types or 'levels' according to their performance and cost[1]:

- the field network – a low level, low cost network for linking small devices such as intelligent sensors, actuators and unitary controllers
- the controller or automation network – a more powerful network that interconnects devices such as HVAC controllers and user interfaces forming part of a building management system
- the system interconnection or management network – a local area network (LAN) for interconnecting different systems within a building, for example HVAC control systems, security systems and fire alarm systems
- the building interconnection network – a wide area network (WAN) for linking buildings together over large distances.

■ 1.2 Protocol layers

The Open System Interconnection (OSI) reference model (ISO standard 7498) defines a design template for data communications standards. The model comprises seven functional 'layers': Physical, Data Link, Network, Transport, Session, Presentation and Application. Each layer corresponds to a specific function or service in data communications. The aim of the standard is to enable everyone participating in an information network to share resources freely, over any distance and in any form. Standards are needed to define the protocols for implementing the functions of all the layers. Products that comply with the same set of OSI standards will be able to communicate without the need for special 'gateways'.

Protocols like Ethernet and Token Ring implement the lower layers of the model and are concerned, for example, with how information is converted into electrical signals, encoded into bits of data, and passed from one device to another. Protocols like BACnet implement the highest layers and are concerned with management functions such as security, privacy and authority. The LonTalk protocol implements all seven layers.

For a particular application, a number of protocols may be needed to cover all layers of the OSI model and all communications levels. For example, LonTalk, Ethernet and BACnet are among protocols that have been chosen by CEN/TC247 for the field, automation and management levels in building management system applications[2].

For devices to be able to communicate (for example to share temperature readings), they must speak a common language as well as comply with the same protocols. Standards like BACnet and LonTalk, therefore, not only cover the application layer of the OSI model, but they also specify the communications language. The language is specified in terms of 'objects', an example of an object being an input channel for measuring temperature (see Section 2.9).

❑ 2 Review of protocols

■ 2.1 Relevant features

The following features of protocol standards are of interest with respect to *Smart Homes*, and where possible are addressed in the individual descriptions of the various buses beginning in Section 2.2 below:

- **Typical applications:** whether intended for use in homes, commercial buildings or factories.
- **Physical layer:** possibilities for using mains signalling (power-lines), copper wiring (including unscreened twisted pair, screened twisted pair, coaxial), optical fibre, cordless infra-red and radio technologies.
- **Main characteristics:** transmission speed (kbit/s), suitability for audio, data and video, topology, maximum number of devices on bus, maximum length, expandability, need for repeaters, and power requirements.
- **Compatibility:** with other protocols, with structured cabling systems[3,4], availability of gateways for interlinking systems, schemes for product certification.
- **Acceptance:** incorporation in European/international standards, adoption by manufacturers and users.
- **Ease of installation:** requirements for cabling and power, opportunities for using structured wiring, need for installation precautions (against electrical interference and for safety).
- **Ease of commissioning:** method of setting device addresses (hardware or software), availability of plug and play, need for user programming.
- **Ease of use:** quality of user interface.
- **Adaptability/expandability:** constraints imposed by power, cabling and network design, existence of third party suppliers of hardware and software, cost.
- **Reliability/robustness:** immunity to electrical interference, use of error correction, complexity of hardware and software, effect of heavy network traffic.
- **Security:** security of data transmission, suitability for use in safety-related applications (for example fire detection), data privacy.
- **Safety:** use of extra low voltage (SELV, PELV or FELV), any restrictions on use in bathrooms and outdoors.
- **Power requirements:** voltage, current, availability of power from bus.
- **Costs:** hardware costs per communications node, and of cabling; costs of system and applications software; costs of maintenance and upgrading.
- **Future developments:** in standardisation, adoption by market.

2.2 BatiBUS

The BatiBUS standard was developed by the French company Merlin Gerin, and is supported by a club (BatiBUS Club International, or BCI) comprising many European companies[5]. It is a simple, low cost bus for field network level communications in homes, offices, schools, hospitals and industrial premises. It has been developed for control of lighting, heating, security, fire detection, hot water and other building services.

The bus is based on twisted pair cable (but with options for infra-red and radio). The bus topology is bus, ring, tree or star. The maximum cable length is 2500 m, with a maximum distance of 600 m between the supply and the farthest point. The transmission rate is 4.8 kbit/s.

Central control of the system bus is from a PC or a special central control unit. The special control unit provides the bus with power (at 15 Vdc) so that devices can be powered directly from the bus. Up to 1000 points can be connected to the bus, with up to 75 powered directly from the bus. There is a maximum of 240 addresses and 24 channels per system. However, a number of systems can be linked together through a so-called J-bus.

The address of each device on the bus can be set in hardware or software. Groupe Schneider has chosen to use thumb-wheels on its products, which are accessible without the use of a tool.

Disconnection or omission of a device does not affect the system's integrity. The system also has collision detection.

2.3 EIB

The European Installation Bus is, like BatiBUS, a standard for field network level communications[5]. It was originally developed by a number of German companies, but is now supported by an association (the EIBA) of European companies. It is designed to operate in both homes and large commercial buildings, with or without a central bus manager. Applications include control of HVAC, lighting, shutters, and monitoring and supervision.

EIB is based on twisted pair cable, with a tree structure consisting of a backbone and 12 branch lines, each up to 1 km long. Up to 64 devices can be connected to a branch line. The transmission rate is 9.6 kbit/s. Further expansion and links to other systems are possible. The system has collision detection. Busch-Jaeger have now released a power-line solution for EIB.

System programming is carried out through a PC or hand-held controller. Device addresses are set in software. A 24 Vdc supply is available on the bus to power devices. Inductors are used to condition the transmission line and prevent the power supply providing a low impedance path at signalling frequencies.

Unscreened twisted pair cable may be run in power trunking without electrical interference. This is due to the pulsing method of bus signalling which gives a high level of immunity to common mode noise. Shielded double twisted pair cable should be used for long cable runs.

A product certification scheme exists to ensure compatibility between products from different manufacturers.

■ 2.4 EHS

The European Home Systems bus (EHS) was developed by Philips, Thomson and AEG as part of a European funded Esprit II project[6]. The Esprit bus is the most comprehensive of the European home buses[7] in that it provides for the control and monitoring of energy management systems, lighting, fire and security systems, voice and data communication, entertainment equipment and domestic appliances. EHS is the only bus that includes video at present, but in analogue form.

Data transmission can be along power-lines, twisted pair cable, screened twisted pair cable, coaxial cable, or plastic optical fibre, or transmission can be cordless by infra-red or radio. Power for devices is available from the copper media. The transmission rate depends on the medium, varying from 0.6 kbit/s for radio to 9.6 kbit/s for unscreened twisted pair. Using unscreened twisted pair cable, the maximum length of cable is 500 m, and the maximum number of devices is 128. These figures are reduced for screened cables.

Further development of the bus is under the control of the European Home Standards Association (EHSA)[8]. In particular, work is underway to merge EHS with BatiBus and EIB (see section 3 below).

■ 2.5 European Process Fieldbus

A number of protocols have been developed for use in industrial process control applications at the field and automation network levels[9]. The protocols are also suitable for building automation applications, although they are likely to be more expensive solutions than the buses described so far, which are aimed mainly at commercial buildings and homes.

The most highly developed of the process field bus protocols is Profibus, which was developed in Germany[10]. It uses screened or unscreened twisted pair cable at transmission rates of 9.6 to 1.5 Mbit/s. An enhanced version of Profibus has also been developed that offers a transmission rate of 12 Mbit/s. Three versions of Profibus now exist: Profibus-FMS for universal application at the field and automation level, and Profibus-DP and Profibus-PA which are optimised for the field level. Options are available for powering devices from the bus and for intrinsically safe operation.

In March 1996, Profibus-FMS and Profibus-DP were ratified as part of European Standard EN 50170, which covers factory, process and building automation. EN 50170 also includes two other national field buses, the Danish P-NET and the French WorldFIP. In Europe all public procurements for process control applications will now be based on EN 50170 field buses. IEC standardisation work on field buses has been underway for more than 10 years, but only the Physical layer has so far been ratified. The recently set up Fieldbus Foundation is now working towards producing a single, integrated standard for industrial process applications[11].

A certification scheme exists for Profibus products to give users the security that devices from different manufacturers will communicate together on the same bus. To receive a Profibus certificate, a device must pass conformance and interoperability tests at an accredited test laboratory. Currently, more than 100 Profibus products from various manufacturers have been certified.

■ 2.6 LonWorks

Developed by the Echelon Corporation, the LonWorks network is designed to provide communications over a variety of physical media for a wide range of products and systems in building automation and other networked, distributed control applications[5,9,12]. Over 2000 companies now have or are developing LonWorks products. Echelon supply all the hardware and software tools needed to develop applications.

The network protocol, LonTalk, is implemented in a dedicated integrated circuit, the Neuron chip, manufactured for Echelon by Motorola and Toshiba. LonTalk implements all seven layers of the OSI model, using a mixture of hardware and firmware on the Neuron chip. Included are services such as sender authentication, priority transmissions, duplicate message detection, collision avoidance, automatic retries, mixed data rates, and error detection and recovery.

LonTalk supports twisted pair wiring, power-line wiring, radio frequency and infra-red communication, as well as coaxial and fibre optics media. The maximum transmission rate is 1.25 Mbit/s.

A LonWorks network can have up to 32,000 nodes, where each node may be, for example, a proximity sensor, switch, motion detector, relay, motor drive, instrument or building controller. Communication may be peer-to-peer or master-slave.

A variety of techniques are used to achieve reliable operation. The protocol allows successful receipt of a message to be acknowledged, and all packet transmissions include a full 16 bit error polynomial. Transceivers for electrically noisy media incorporate forward error correction that can detect and correct single bit errors without the need for retransmission. The Neuron chip also contains self-test circuitry, three watchdog timers and a variety of diagnostic features such as EEPROM memory corruption check.

The protocol is an enhancement of the CSMA technique used by Ethernet, which provides a linear response with traffic load, predictable response times for heavily loaded networks, and performance independent of network size.

The LonTalk protocol incorporates a full set of network management functions, including node address assignment, network diagnostics, etc. Every packet transmission can also invoke a sender authenticity function.

Product interoperability (see Section 0) is ensured by:

- encapsulating as many features as possible into the chip
- incorporating standard types and objects into the technology so that products agree on the meaning of shared data
- the existence of an independent body to manage the evolution of the interoperability model.

A product certification scheme has been established based on a LonMark logo to indicate that a product has passed conformance tests and complies with LonMark interoperability guidelines.

The Electronics Industry Association has published LonWorks as an EIA standard for home automation – EIA 709. Additionally, the protocol is referenced in the ASHRAE (American Society of Heating, Refrigeration, and Air Conditioning Engineers) BACnet control standard for buildings.

Echelon hardware is now becoming available from other sources, and LonTalk may be implemented on non-Neuron chips, although a fee is required for a unique chip ID.

■ 2.7 X10

X10 is a simple, low cost protocol developed in the USA for home automation over power-lines[13]. It dates from 1977, and products have been developed since then for a wide range of simple home automation applications, including switching devices on and off and dimming lights. Up to 256 devices can be addressed. However, most communications are one way only from the controller to the device, so that receipt and recognition of a command cannot be verified. To improve reliability, data bits are sent twice.

■ 2.8 CEBus

The Consumer Electronics Bus, CEBus, was developed by the US Electronic Industries Association for residential applications, and is specified in the standard EIA-600[13]. CEBus provides a special language for home automation functions, and uses a proprietary signalling method devised by the CEBus committee[14] that operates at 6.7 kbit/s. Data transmission can be over power-lines, coaxial cable, twisted pair, infra-red or radio.

Data transmission over power-lines using CEBus is based on 'spread spectrum' signalling for improved reliability. However, the bandwidth extends to 400 kHz, which rules this out as an option in Europe where the maximum allowed band for consumer power-line applications is 95 to 148.5 kHz (with most companies operating in the 'access-control' band of 125 to 140 kHz).

The protocol uses 4 layers of the OSI model, namely the Physical, Link, Network and Application layers. The communications hardware and protocol are available as an Intellon integrated circuit, and other components are available for interfacing to power-lines and radio.

■ 2.9 BACnet

Developed by ASHRAE, BACnet specifies a suite of communications protocols and a comprehensive set of messages for connecting together building automation components from different manufacturers[15]. It can be used at the field, controller and management levels, by smart sensors and actuators, unitary controllers, programmable controllers, and central computers.

The protocols specified by BACnet are the LANs Ethernet, Arcnet, MS/TP and LonTalk, and the serial interface EIA-232[16]. The content of the messages, the BACnet language, is the major part of the standard. The language is specified in terms of 'objects', 'properties' and 'services' based on a sophisticated model for describing all types of building automation systems. Altogether there are 18 objects, each of which has a standard set of properties. For example, one standard object is the 'analogue input' object (traditionally referred to as a 'point' in the building controls industry). Its properties include 'description' (for example 'outside temperature'), 'device type' (for example 'themistor'), 'present value' (for example '21'), and 'units' (for example 'degrees C'). Altogether, there are 123 properties of objects.

Services are the means by which one BACnet device acquires information from another device, commands another device to perform certain actions, or announces to one or more devices that some event has taken place. For example, a display device could request the 'outside temperature' object to return its 'present value'. BACnet defines 32 services.

BACnet was adopted by ANSI in December 1995 (ANSI/ASHRAE 135-1995), and it is now under review by the International Standards Organisation (ISO). Standard Microsystems Corporation (SMC) recently announced a single chip implementation of Arcnet (ANSI 878.1), one of the LAN protocols specified in BACnet, which is designed specifically for embedded control in BACnet-based building control applications at speeds from 156 kbit/s to 5 Mbit/s.

■ 2.10 FND

Developed by the German public authorities, FND (Firm Neutral Data transmission) is a standard for building to building communications. It implements the Application layer of the OSI Model, and requires the use of gateways (based on the CCITT standards X.21 and X.25) onto a local or wide area network.

■ 2.11 ISO LAN standards

Four common LAN standards are dealt with by ISO 8802: Ethernet (ISO 8802/3), Token Ring (ISO 8802/5), Token Bus (ISO 8802/4) and Slotted Ring (ISO 8802/7).

Ethernet is the most popular for building management and control applications, and can be used at the automation and management levels of building control. It was originally developed jointly by DEC, Intel and Rank Xerox for general office, retail, banking and factory use. The transmission speed is up to 10 Mbit/s over coaxial or twisted pair cable, although 4 Mbit/s is the limit for long packets, and performance with short packets is very poor due to the inter-packet gaps. Systems that operate at speeds of up to 100 Mbit/s over Category 5 twisted pair cable are also available.

■ 2.12 ATM

Asynchronous Transfer Mode (ATM) was originally developed for use by the telecommunications industry as a long-distance 'backbone' protocol, but is being adopted increasingly by businesses as a high performance local area network[17]. It may have applications in linking *Smart Homes* to control centres where security of transmission is vital (for example to report the outbreak of a fire or serious illness).

ATM offers significant benefits when compared with alternative networking technologies. It is supported by the ATM Forum, an industry-wide group comprising suppliers and users, which has become the de facto standards making body of the ATM industry. Compatible equipment is readily available from a range of suppliers.

ATM transmits data in fixed length blocks comprising 48 bytes of data and a 5 byte header, a form of packet structure used by other protocols such as Ethernet. However, whereas with Ethernet no communication takes place between the sending and receiving terminals before data are transmitted, with ATM there is first a call set up phase to define the connection path. With this technique, data transmission speeds greater than 1 Gbit/s can be achieved. Unlike Ethernet, ATM also copes well with large numbers of users.

The feature that makes ATM unique is that existing standards specify five service levels. These range from low speed, constant bit rate applications such as voice, to high speed, bursty applications such as file transfer between a server and a client. The quality of service across an ATM network can therefore be controlled. Ethernet, Token Ring and FDDI networks do not distinguish between critical data and non-critical data. For example, the transmission of a CAD image or a multi-million pound banking transaction can be delayed by someone playing games or browsing the Internet. ATM can guarantee that voice and video are delivered simultaneously with minimal jitter, and are not interrupted by, say, e-mail. ATM is thus ideally suited to multimedia applications.

The final attraction of ATM is its scalability. Using ATM, data packets can be transmitted at whatever speed is appropriate. With existing networks, the technology has to change as the transmission speed increases – for example serial line to Ethernet, Ethernet to FDDI, FDDI to HPPI. In contrast, existing ATM equipment can support data rates ranging from 2 Mbit/s for low speed wide area networks, through to 25 Mbit/s and 155 Mbit/s for desktop workstation connections, and up to 2.5 Gbit/s for backbones.

❑ 3 Progress on European standardisation of protocols for homes and buildings

■ 3.1 Merger of European buses

An important recent development has been the agreement to merge BatiBUS, EIB and EHS into a new HBES standard, known for the moment as the 'Convergence' protocol. Work on harmonising the standards is being led by the European Homes Systems Association (EHSA) with the support of the companies Schneider and Seimens.

There are technical difficulties in merging the standards due to fundamental differences in the basic structure of the protocols. For example, whereas EIB is 'data driven', EHS is 'command-based'. Also, they use fundamentally different addressing mechanisms, and EHS is not currently very suitable for large installations. Nevertheless, the plan is that BatiBUS and EIB will both be compatible with the new Convergence protocol and will continue to be supported by Schneider and Seimens.

A detailed draft specification was submitted to the members of BCI, EIBA and EHSA in March 1998, and the final version of the specification is now nearing completion. The first products incorporating the Convergence protocol are scheduled to be released in 1999, and Landis & Staefa and Honeywell Centra have confirmed that they will shortly release certified products.

■ 3.2 Activity within CEN/CENELEC

Two European standardisation committees are working on protocol standards for building automation. CEN committee TC247 is developing standards for controls for mechanical building services, including building management systems, for use principally in commercial buildings, while CENELEC (CLC) TC205 is developing standards for home and building electronic systems.

Both committees are in the process of choosing communications protocols for inclusion in their standards. CEN/TC247 has made more progress than CLC/TC205, although it has not been able to settle on just one protocol for each of the field, automation and management levels. Instead the CEN/TC247 standard will contain a list of protocols from which manufacturers and users will choose the ones most suited to their application. Table A2.1 (from reference 2) summarises the present state of CEN/TC247's standard.

CEN/TC247 is now working on the definition of common objects for the selected protocols. The management and controller level protocols FND and Profibus already have a subset of the BACnet objects. Field level objects are much more basic, since they cover communications between simple devices like sensors and actuators rather than with a user interface or central station. CEN/TC247 and CLC/TC205 are working together to write a common set of object definitions for field level protocols. These will be related to the objects used at other levels, particularly by BACnet.

It will be some time before it will be possible to 'mix and match' components from different manufacturers of building services systems[2]. At the moment, building a system with components from different manufacturers is likely to compromise system performance and increase engineering time. Once object definitions have been agreed, the problems of linking different protocols will become easier. In the meantime, Table A2.2 indicates how good compatibility can be achieved for systems constructed using the levels concept, and so that networks can 'co-exist' sharing a common cabling system.

Table A2.1 CEN/TC247 selected protocols for HVAC control systems

Level	Objects	Transmission	Source	Standard
Management	FND	X25 to FND network access unit	Germany	ENV 1805-2: 1996
	BACnet	PSTN/dial up modem Ethernet – 10 Mbit/s	ASHRAE, USA	ENV 1805-1: 1998
Automation	Profibus	Profibus FMS – twisted pair – 9.6 kbit/s to 1.5 Mbit/s	Germany	ENV 13321-1: 1999
	WorldFIP	WorldFIP – twisted pair – 31.25 kbit/s to 2.5 Mbit/s	France	ENV 13321-1: 1999
	BACnet	PSTN/dial up modem Ethernet – 10 Mbit/s LonTalk – 1.25 Mbit/s or 78 kbit/s	ASHRAE, USA	ENV 13321-1: 1999
	EIB	EIB – twisted pair – 9.6 kbit/s	EIBA, Germany	Draft ENV 13321-2
Field	EIB	EIB – twisted pair – 9.6 kbit/s	EIBA, Germany	ENV 13154-2: 1998
	BatiBUS	BatiBUS – twisted pair – 4.8 kbit/s	BCI, France	ENV 13154-2: 1998
	LonWorks	LonTalk – twisted pair – 78 kbit/s	Echelon, USA	ENV 13154-2: 1998
	EHS	Various media	Europe	ENV 13154-2: 1998

Table A2.2 Examples of protocols for compatibility in building management systems applications

	Poor compatibility	Good compatibility
Management	FND	BACnet over Ethernet
Automation	BACnet	BACnet over LONtalk
Field	BatiBUS	LONworks over LONtalk

'Coexistence' is just the first step to full 'interoperability'. With coexistence, different systems can send private messages over the same network cabling. In this way, infrastructure costs are shared, and, moreover, system development is not constrained by standardisation. 'Interworking' is the second step, in which there is transmission of selected values between different systems in an open way. 'Interoperability' is the final step, in which products communicate completely openly in accordance with a standard protocol. The main benefit is the ability to choose system components from different manufacturers, although the disadvantages are that system engineering becomes more difficult and innovation may be inhibited.

❑ 4 Structured wiring

A 'structured wiring system' is an integrated cabling system for all the electronic and computer systems in a building[4]. The structured wiring may comprise a selection of different types of cable including unscreened twisted pair and co-axial cable installed along common trunking, conduit or cable trays. The cables may carry signals for voice, data, building control, fire, security, home entertainment and video. Special wall outlets provide a convenient means of making connections in any part of a building to the desired technical system. All incoming signals are routed through a central wiring closet. Power cabling is kept separate from the structured wiring.

It is suggested that a structured wiring system will reduce the initial construction costs for a commercial building by up to 30%. It also gives the building the ability to adapt and respond quickly and easily to the changing requirements of building users, cutting the cabling related costs of 'churn' by up to 60%. For homes, although initial wiring costs may be higher, structured wiring provides a convenient way of accommodating future smart systems.

The international standard for structured wiring is IEC 11801. Two commercially available US products are AMP's OnQ and Lucent's Homestar.

❑ 5 Residential gateways

The transmission within, and to and from, homes of digital data, video and other signals is being addressed by both CENELEC committee CLC/TC205 and the IEEE in the US (standardisation projects P1355 and P1394).

Consideration is being given to the need for an 'electronic consumer unit' – or 'residential gateway' – for the different types of digital data, to decode, encode, and route the signals to their destination.

Current thinking is that high-speed, broadband data (for example video and ATM) should be kept separate from low-speed control and information data (for example power-line and BatiBUS). The residential gateway provides a point of contact for the broadband and narrow band signals so that, for example, commands can be sent from a video screen to a washing machine, or devices can send information to the screen.

The chosen communications protocols will determine the type of residential gateway needed. Whether the gateway can be a simple router or must be a more complex 'application gateway' will depend on the underlying structure of the protocols, as well as on requirements for maintaining safety and security. The complexity of the gateway needed can be used as a criterion for selecting communications protocols.

ATM could in principle be used as a common network for high speed and low speed data to and from *Smart Homes*, but it is too expensive for use within homes.

❑ 6 Analysis and discussion

The X-10, CEBus and FND protocols will be excluded from further consideration in this paper. The X-10 bus is very low cost, but communication is in only one direction and reliability and security are inherently very poor. CEBus is a technology that has been developed for the US market, it is not being considered by CLC/TC205 or CEN/TC247, and the standard power-line option does not comply with European regulations. FND is unique to Germany.

■ 6.1 Comparison of features of main protocols

Table A2.3 presents a comparison of the main protocols with potential for application within and between *Smart Homes*. The table is intended to be used as a basis for further discussion with system manufacturers and suppliers, and may change in the light of feedback.

An explanation of the terms used in the 'features' column is given in Section 2.1. The application areas (homes, commercial buildings, factories) are given in order of potential market size. All other features are given a rating between 1 and 5, where 5 is 'best' (for example highest performance, lowest cost).

The protocols most suitable for use within *Smart Homes* are the field level (and possibly controller level) protocols. These are the lowest cost (and lowest performance) network protocols, but apart from EHS make no provision for video.

Table A2.3 Comparison of features of main protocols

Feature	Protocol							
	BatiBUS	EIB	EHS	Profibus	LonTalk/ LonWorks BACnet	Ethernet/ BACnet	PSTN/ BACnet	ATM/ BACnet
Application	C, H, F	C, H, F	C, H, F	F, C	C, H, F	C	C, F, H	C
Performance	1	2	2	3, 4	3	4	4	5
Range of media	3	2	5	2	5	2	2	2
Compatibility	3	5	3	5	5	5	5	5
Acceptance	2	2	1	3	3	5	5	3
Ease of installation	3	3	3	3	3	3	3	3
Ease of commissioning	3	3	3	3	3	3	3	3
Ease of use	3	3	3	3	3	3	3	3
Adaptability	3	3	3	3	3	3	3	3
Reliability	2	3	2	4	3	5	1	5
Security	3	3	3	5	5	5	5	5
Safety	3	3	3	5	3	3	3	3
Power requirements	5	5	5	5	5	3	1	1
Costs	5	4	4	3	4	2	3	1

■ 6.2 The views of the market

Within Europe, the main battle in commercial buildings at the field and controller level is between the BatiBUS/EIB/EHS group of protocols, LonWorks, and the European process control bus Fieldbus.

The future of BatiBUS and EIB is uncertain following the agreement between Schneider and Siemens to merge the buses in a new version of EHS, known as the 'convergence' protocol. It is not yet clear that all the technical problems can be overcome. However, there is significant support among manufacturers for the buses, especially in France and Germany where BatiBUS and EIB have large markets. Electrolux is apparently committed to using the new EHSA protocol in future domestic products. Landis & Staefa and Honeywell Centra have announced that they will launch certified products shortly.

In the UK and Scandinavia, LonWorks appears to be the favourite among consultants and manufacturers of building control systems for commercial buildings. It is believed that most of the major European controls companies are gearing up to provide LonWorks as an option to users, and new companies such as SeaChange have adopted LonWorks exclusively.

The European Fieldbus is supported by a large number of process control companies throughout Europe. However, process control products have traditionally been significantly more expensive than building control products.

The view of many – but by no means all – in the building controls industry is that LonWorks is becoming the de facto standard for commercial buildings in the UK. The technical performance of the buses is not the main issue as they all work, although they all have advantages, disadvantages and problems. The main concern is that everyone should agree to use the same protocol.

❑ 7 Conclusions

Developments in standardisation of communications protocols suitable for *Smart Homes* and buildings are still taking place.

Of the field and controller level buses, the European Fieldbus (Profibus) is the first to become part of a European standard, but it is primarily intended for industrial process control applications, and may be too expensive and over-engineered for home applications.

The field level buses BatiBUS, EIB, EHS and LonWorks are all close to becoming recognised as European standards for environmental control applications (heating, ventilation and air conditioning). The future of the first three is a little uncertain following the decision of BCI, EIBA and EHSA in February 1997 to begin a 'process of convergence' leading to a new version of EHS. The first products incorporating the 'Convergence' protocol are scheduled to become available in 1999. Landis & Staefa and Honeywell

Centra have already confirmed that they will launch certified products shortly. It looks likely that, if the convergence work is successful, the Convergence protocol will share the homes and commercial buildings markets in Europe with LonWorks.

In the UK commercial buildings sector, the view of many in the UK controls industry is that LonWorks is now becoming the de facto standard.

If the different systems in buildings are to be able to communicate, they must not only comply with the same protocols, but they must also speak the same language. Languages are specified in terms of 'objects', and the most comprehensive set of objects is contained in BACnet, which is now a European ENV standard. Profibus and FND already contain a subset of the BACnet objects. Work by CEN/TC247 and CLC/TC205 on defining a common set of BACnet-compatible objects for their field level protocols is nearing completion. It will not be possible to 'mix and match' components from different manufacturers of building services systems – that is to achieve full 'interoperability' – until these object definitions have been agreed.

Transmission of digital video requires a high bandwidth network like Ethernet or ATM working over Category 5 twisted pair cable or coaxial cable. Of the home and building buses, only EHS has been designed to carry video, but in an analogue rather than digital form. It is likely that, for the foreseeable future, video will be kept separate from low speed control and information data. Structured wiring systems can provide separate cables for video and other types of data. However, there is then a requirement for a 'residential gateway' or 'electronic consumer unit' to route signals between, say, video screens and other devices like washing machines on the field bus.

An application of ATM may be to link *Smart Homes* to control centres where security of transmission is vital (for example to report the outbreak of a fire or serious illness).

❑ 8 References

1 K Bromley. Building IT 2000, pp 152-156. The Building Centre Trust. May 1991.

2 C Chapman. Communications standards – are they finished? *Building Services and Environmental Engineer*, pp 23-26, January 1997.

3 The EOSYS cabling guide for building professionals. *Architects' Journal*, June/July 1988.

4 B Sewell. Structured wiring systems for intelligent buildings. Proceedings of IB/IC Intelligent Buildings Congress, Tel-Aviv, Israel, March 1997.

5 Members guide to home and building electronic systems. Electrical Contractors' Association, July 1992.

6 A technical guide to European Home Systems. Home Systems Components Consortium, December 1994.

7 Waiting for the right bus. *Electrical Contractor*, January 1991.

8 http://www.ehsa.com

9 Protocol roundup. HPAC, *Connectivity*, February 1997.

10 http://www.profibus.com

11 G Wool. Regulation updates for the thinking, feeling building. IEEIE, January 1997.

12 http://www.echelon.com

13 M Yomura. Analysis of building automation systems. Proceedings of IB/IC Intelligent Buildings Congress, Tel-Aviv, Israel, March 1997.

14 http://www.cebus.com

15 W Swan. The language of BACnet. *Engineered Systems Magazine*, 1996.

16 W Swan. Internetworking with BACnet. *Engineered Systems Magazine*, 1997.

17 N Squibb. Networking à la mode. *IEE Review*, January 1997.

APPENDIX 3

EUROPEAN *SMART HOME* RESEARCH AND DEVELOPMENT PROJECTS

A number of projects across Europe are exploring the possibilities of emerging *Smart Home* technologies. Several are investigating the provision of services to the elderly and people with disabilities. The social groups targeted by this research and development activity vary considerably (see Table A3.1). The following listings are by no means comprehensive, but provide an indication of other demonstration work in the field.

■ Portsmouth

The Portsmouth *Smart Home* project is a joint research project with the following partners: Portsmouth City Council; The University of Portsmouth; and John Grooms Housing Association. With funding from the Housing Corporation, the project aims to produce design solutions to assist people with disabilities to live independently. A total of six units are to be built in Portsmouth using these designs. The project will examine the use of *Smart Homes* technologies in conjunction with architectural solutions. As new build properties the design will incorporate ways to include the additional cabling and motor equipment required by *Smart Home* systems. Of the six dwellings only three will actually have the additional electronics installed at construction stage. The project is currently in the design stage with designs being evaluated by potential user groups in the Portsmouth area prior to construction.

■ Integer

The INTEGER (Intelligent and Green) project has its roots in a conceptual design prepared by Cole Thompson Associates for the DTI UK Now exhibition in November 1997. INTEGER now comprises over 150 partner organisations and is promoting 'intelligent technology for managing the systems within the home and for communications to and from the home'.

INTEGER were asked, based on the conceptual design, to build a demonstration house by the BBC which was filmed during construction and broadcast in early 1999.

The house utilised a variety of smart devices and protocols (EIB for lighting, Echelon for heating and access control, and EHS for whitegoods control) to improve control, comfort, safety and security for the occupants as well as assist in energy conservation. The choice of protocols was based on those suppliers prepared to donate products to the project.

INTEGER are trying to apply these ideas to affordable housing. They are currently working on plans for around 100 social housing units on sites in West Bromwich, Harlow, Maidenhead and North Wiltshire with construction expected next year. Refurbishment of existing properties is being examined as a research area for INTEGER in the future.

■ Rice Homes

Rice Homes, a speculative house builder based in Hertfordshire is examining the market potential of installing small home networks in new built homes. Based on a system developed by ITT Cannon, the network consists of CAT 5 cabling to multiple sockets in each room linked at a patch panel. This network can be used to carry computer data, video images, sound from the stereo, and telephony, with each socket able to carry out any function and be altered by the user as required.

■ Anchor

The Anchor Trust has been carrying out research in collaboration with British Telecom to examine the use of ICTs as a monitoring and emergency alert system for elderly people. The system uses movement, heat, and contact sensors to monitor the level of activity in the dwelling. This information is recorded in a control box attached to the telephone. On a regular basis this information is remotely downloaded and analysed. Over time, a pattern of activity is developed which can then be checked and in the case of an abnormal activity period (e.g. lack of movement at a time expected) alert carers. Carer alert is again handled by the remote system and can page through a number of carers by telephone until one of them confirms that they are able to respond to the alert. The system is currently on trial on a number of sites across the UK.

■ RESO

This brings together organisations from across Europe, including social housing providers, industry, research establishments, advocacy groups and technical consultants.

The individual demonstration sites are platforms for the introduction of integrated services in health care, household assistance, security, meal delivery, and minor repairs, as well as the information and communications services. The Vällingby demonstrator (Hunhammar 1996), for example, is testing videophone services between flats and the district housing office, and between flats and the communal entrance, and electronic bulletin board controlled by the janitor and tenants, and an automatic booking system for the communal laundry facility, with remote monitoring of the progress of the washing cycle. A building access system connected to the lift and the doorkey is also being tested.

Specific groups targeted by the RESO projects have been derived from interviews with user groups, individual users, and professionals. The Vällingby scheme, for example, is exploring technologies which are able to cope with the changing needs of six groups of older and disabled people with contrasting daily living requirements (see Hjælpemiddelinstituttet, no date):

1. Older people living at home
2. Older people in sheltered accommodation
3. Older people in nursing homes
4. Physically disabled people living at home
5. Physically disabled people in shared accommodation
6. People with brain damage in care institutions.

■ Majala, Finland

A major scheme at Majala in Joensuu (Routio 1996) involves the construction of new homes which are adaptable to the changing needs of *all* residents. No specific homes for people with disabilities will be built, as each dwelling is planned and constructed to promote flexibility and accessibility. As well as the inclusion of lifetime homes concepts, the scheme involves the implementation of teleworking systems to benefit people who have difficulties in reaching their offices. Public information and teleshopping services have been designed for maximum accessibility.

Table A3.1 Examples of other European Smart Home research and development projects

Project	Target groups/needs	*Smart Home* applications
RESO Programme: Vällingby (Sweden), Chateauroux (France), Almere (Netherlands)	Elderly and disabled people resident in social housing. Aims to improve quality of life via user-friendly home services based on telecommunication media.	Integrated services in health care, household assistance, security, meal delivery, minor repairs, and information and communications services.
HS-ADEPT project (TIDE Programme, Project 1102)	Disabled and older people. Integrated home systems to offer improved access and control of the domestic environment.	
RACE project (Germany, Netherlands, Italy, Sweden, Finland and Portugal)	Elderly and disabled people. Community care applications of videotelephony.	Includes alarm services and physiotherapy.
Örebro (Sweden)	Young people with physical disabilities. Shared accommodation with technical aids.	Integrated technical solutions with full functional control.
ESPACE XXI (France)	People with multiple physical disabilities.	
Ler-bo (Denmark)	Older people with injuries caused by falling.	Solutions are limited to controlling lights, curtains, and venetian blinds, and simple switch control.
'Sophie's House' (Denmark)	Exhibition house designed to test technical aids for older and disabled persons.	
Majala (Joensuu, Finland)	All population groups. Construction of new homes which are adaptable to changing household needs.	Lifetime homes concepts, teleworking systems to benefit people who have difficulties in reaching their offices, public information and teleshopping services designed for maximum accessibility.

Appendix 4

Bibliography

Abercrombie, N., Hill, S. and Turner, B.S. (1986) *Sovereign Individuals of Capitalism*, London, Allen & Unwin.

Abramson, P. and Ingelhart, R. (1995) *Value Change in Global Perspective*, Ann Arbor, University of Michigan Press.

Bannert, M. and Kunkel, K. (1991) 'What can be learned from research in human-computer interaction?', *European Review of Applied Psychology*, Vol. 41, No. 4, pp. 271-278.

Barlow, J. (1999) 'From craft production to mass customisation. Innovation requirements for the UK housebuilding industry', *Housing Studies*, Vol. 14, No. 1.

Barlow, J. and Gann, D.M. (1998) 'A Changing Sense of Place: are integrated IT systems reshaping the home?', presented at *Technological Futures, Urban Futures* Conference, Durham, 23-24 April 1998.

Barrow, M. and Bachan, R. (1997) *The Real Cost of Poor Homes: Footing the Bill: How Poor Quality Housing Affects the Lives of Residents and Service Providers*, A Report prepared for the Royal Institution of Chartered Surveyors, London.

Bedrosian, M. and Bedrosian, A. (1994) 'Technology in the home: a benefit/cost analysis', in Bjerk, K. and Borreby, K. (eds.) *Proceedings of the International Working Conference on Home-Oriented Informatics, Telematics and Automation*. University of Copenhagen, 27 June – 1 July.

Birnbaum, J. (1999) *After the Internet*, London, The Royal Academy of Engineering.

Bjørneby, S. (Ed.) (1994) *Technology for Independent Living in Life Cycle Housing*, Proceedings from the BESTA International Conference, 8-9 June 1994, Oslo, Norway.

BMA (1995) *Taking care of the carers*, February, p. 3.

Brech, J and Potter, P (eds.) (1994) *Growing Older In The Community: European Projects In Housing And Planning*, London, Anchor Housing Trust.

Bright, J. (1996) *Lifetime Homes: Built today, designed for tomorrow*, York, Joseph Rowntree Foundation.

Buckby, S. (1998) 'Care homes regulator planned', *Financial Times*, September 25, p. 9.

Burley, R. (1994) 'Towards a house building technology for the adaptable smarter home', presented at the BESTA International Conference, *Technology for Independent Living in Life Cycle Homes*, Lillehammer, Norway, 8-9 June.

Burley, R. (1998) 'Ideal homes?', *Managing Care*, December, p. 18.

Castells, M. (1989) *The Informational City. Information Technology, Economic Restructuring and the Urban-Regional Process*, Oxford, Basil Blackwell.

Castells, M. (1998) *The Information Age. Economy, Society and Culture. Vol. I-III*, Oxford, Basil Blackwell.

Cawson, A. and Lewis, J. (1999) *A report summarising academic research and public domain market research on attitudes to and use of Information Technologies in the Home*, prepared for the DTI by SIMI, Brighton.

Construction Industry Board (1998) *Strategic Review of Construction Skills Training*, London, Thomas Telford Publishing.

Cullen, K. and Moran, R. (1991) *Technology and the Elderly*, Dublin, EKOS.

Dard, P. (1996) 'Dilemmas of telesurveillance in housing', Paper presented at the ENHR Housing Conference, Helsingør, August.

Devries, G., Vangelderen, T. and Brigham, F. (1994) 'Usability laboratories at Philips – supporting research, development, and design for consumer and professional products', *Behaviour & Information Technology*, Vol. 13, No. 1-2, pp. 119-127.

Dicken, P. (1992) *Global Shift. The Internationalisation of Economic Activity*, London, Paul Chapman.

DOE (1995) *Projections of Households in England to 2016*, London, HMSO.

Doughty, K. Cameron, K. and Garner, P. (1996) 'Three generations of telecare of the elderly', *Journal of Telemedicine and Telecare*, Vol. 2, pp. 71-80.

Doughty, K. and Williams, A. (1999) 'Smart Sensors for Application in Integrated Telecare Systems', paper presented at *Hospitals Without Walls Conference*, City University, London, March 24-26.

Drage, G. (1997) 'What should we as an industry be doing at this stage of market development?' Paper presented at the Intelligent Living Conference, Hanover, 10-11 November 1997.

ESPRIT-HS Consortium (1991) *Home System Specification*, ESPRIT Home Systems project 2431.

European Commission (1994) *Technology initiative for disabled and elderly people*, TIDE, Directorate General XIII.

Forester, T. (1989) 'The myth of the electronic cottage', in T. Forester (ed.) *Computers in the Human Context: Information Technology, Productivity and People*, Oxford, Blackwell, pp. 213-227.

Forty, A. (1986) *Objects of Desire: Design and Society 1750-1980*, London, Thames and Hudson.

Gann, D.M. (1992a) *Intelligent Building Technologies: Japan and Singapore*, Department of Trade and Industry Expert Mission Visit Report, SPRU, University of Sussex.

Gann, D.M. (1992b) *Intelligent Buildings – Producers and Users*, Brighton, SPRU, University of Sussex.

Gann, D.M., Iwashita, S., Tidd, J. and Barlow, J. (1994) *Housing and Home Automation for the Elderly and Disabled: scoping study*, SPRU and the Electrical Contractors' Association.

Gann, D.M., Iwashita, I., Barlow, J. and Mandeville, L. (1995) *Housing and Home Automation for People with Disabilities and the Elderly*, for Electrical Contractors' Association. and Atias Corp (Japan), SPRU, University of Sussex.

Gann, D.M., Tang, P. and Curry, R. (1998) *Feasibility Study: Technologies for Telecare in the Home*, working paper, SPRU, University of Sussex, December.

Gann, D.M. (1999) *Flexibility and Choice in Housing*, Bristol, Policy Press.

Gann, D.M., Tang, P. and Curry, R. (1999 forthcoming) *Technologies for Telecare in the home*, Brighton, SPRU, University of Sussex.

Gates, B. (1999) *Business @ the speed of thought: using a digital nervous system*, London, Penguin Books.

George, H. (1995) *The Good Usability Handbook*. London, McGraw Hill.

Graham, S. and Marvin, S. (1996) *Telecommunications and the City. Electronic Spaces, Urban Places*, London, Routledge.

Grinyer, M. (1999) *Teleworking: A Good Practice Guide*, Coventry, CIH.

Haddon, L. (1996), 'Home Automation: Research Issues', in *The Smart Home: Research Perspectives*, European Media, Technology and Everyday Life Network (EMTEL), Working Paper No. 1, University of Sussex, Brighton, May 1996.

Haddon, L. (no date) 'Developments in the US home automation market', mimeo.

Haddon, L., Karl, I. and Mandeville, E. (no date) 'INTEGER: summary of consumer issues', (mimeo).

Hardyment, C. (1988) *From Mangle to Microwave*, Oxford, Polity Press.

Hawkins, R. Mansell, R. and Skea, J. (eds) (1995) *Standards, Innovation, and Competitiveness: the politics and economics of standards in natural and technical environments*, Aldershot, Edward Elgar Publishers.

Heimer, T. (1995) 'The technological genesis of intelligent homes', in Esser, J. *et al.* (Eds.) *Soziale und ökonomische Konflikte in Standardisierungsprozessen*, Frankfurt am Main.

Hepworth, M. (1989) *The Geography of the Information Economy*, London, Belhaven.

Hillman, J. (1993) *Telelifestyles and the Flexicity: A European Study*, Dublin, European Foundation for the Improvement of Living and Working Conditions.

Hirschman, A. (1982) *Shifting Involvements: Public Interest and Private Action*, Oxford, Blackwell.

Hix, D. (1993) *Developing User Interfaces. Ensuring Usability Through Product and Process*, New York, John Wiley.

Hjælpemiddelinstituttet (no date)*'Smart Home' for aeldre og handicappede.* (English summary). Hjælpemiddelinstituttet, Denmark.

Holtzman, S. (1997) *Digital Mosaics –the aesthetics of cyberspace*, New York, Simon & Schuster.

Hooper, A., Dunmore, K. and Hughes, M. (1998) *Home Alone*, Amersham, The Housing Research Foundation, National House Building Council.

Hunhammar, M. (1996) 'IT-supported residential services – test bed Vällingby', Paper presented at the ENHR Housing Conference, Helsingør, August.

Ingelhart, R. (1990) *Culture Shift in Advanced Industrial Societies*, Princeton, University of Princeton Press.

Jeck, M. (1997) 'How to make the market for the intelligent home', Paper presented at the Intelligent Living Conference, Hanover, 10-11 November 1997.

Johnson, N. (1967) 'Communications', *Science Journal*, October.

Jonscher, C. (1999) *Wiredlife: who are we in the digital age?* Bantom Press.

Kaku, M. (1998) *Visions – how science will revolutionise the twenty-first century*, Oxford, Oxford University Press.

Keinonen, T. (1994) 'Home systems for elderly residents. A usability study', Themes 1/1994. STAKES, Nat. Research & Development Centre for Welfare and Health, Helsinki.

Kerr, P. (1996) *Gridiron*, London, Vintage.

Knight, R. and Gappert, G. (Eds.) (1989) *Cities in a Global Society*, London, Sage.

Lorente, S. (1996) 'The global house: new user opportunities in automation and information', Mimeo, Universidad Politecnica de Madrid.

March, A. (1994) 'Usability – the new dimension of product design', *Harvard Business Review,* Vol. 72, No. 5, pp. 144-149.

Martin, F. (1993) *Every House You'll Ever Need: a design guide for barrier free housing*, Edinburgh, Edinvar Housing Association.

Mason, R. (1983) *Xanadu*, New York, Acropolis Books.

Mason, R. and Jennings, L. (1983) 'The computer home: will tomorrow's housing come alive?' *The Futurist*, Vol. 16, No. 1, p. 35.

McCafferty, P. (1994) *Living Independently. A Study of the Housing Needs of Elderly and Disabled People*, London, HMSO.

Meyer, S. and Schulze, E. (1996) 'The Smart Home in the 1990s. Acceptance and Future Usage in Private Households in Europe', in *The Smart Home: Research Perspectives*, The European Media Technology and Everyday Life Network (EMTEL), Working Paper No. 1, University of Sussex, Brighton.

Miles, I. (1988) *Home Informatics: information technology and the transformation of everyday life*, London, Pinter Publishers.

Miles, I., Rush, H., Turner, K., and Bessant, J. (1988) *Information Horizons*, Aldershot, Edward Elgar.

Mitchell, W. (1995) *City of Bits. Space, Place and the Infobahn*, Boston, MIT Press.

Mollenkopf, H. (1993) *Technical aids in old age. Between acceptance and rejection*, Arbeitsgruppe Sozialberichterstattung, Wissenschaftszentrum Berlin für Sozialforschung.

Moran, R. (1993) *The Electronic Home. Social and Spatial Aspects*, Dublin, European Foundation for the Improvement of Living and Working Conditions.

Mulgan, G. (1991) *Communication and Control: Networks and the New Economies of Communication*, Oxford, Polity Press.

Negroponte, N. (1995) *Being Digital,* New York, Alfred A. Knopf.

Ody, P. (1999) 'On the verge of a retail revolution', *Financial Times Survey – Electronic Business*, March 24.

Palmer, S., Gann, D.M., Adams, C., McCosh, A. and MacFarlane, B. (1998) *House from the rising sun: lessons from the Japanese housing delivery experience*, TRADA Technology Research Report.

Parker, G. (1992) 'Counting care: numbers and types of informal carers', in Twigg, J. (ed.) *Carers Research & Practice*, London, HMSO.

Pentland, A. (1996) 'Smart rooms', *Scientific American*, April, pp. 54-62.

Preece, J. (Ed.) (1993) *A Guide to Usability. Human Factors in Computing,* Wokingham, Addison Wesley.

Reeves, B. and Nass, C. (1996) *The Media Equation – how people treat computers, television, and new media like real people and places*, Cambridge University Press/CSLI.

Robins, K. and Hepworth, M. (1988) 'Electronic spaces: new technologies and the future of cities', *Futures*, April, pp. 155-176.

Routio, R. (1996) 'Adaptable smart homes', Paper presented at the ENHR Housing Conference, Helsingør, August.

Rowlands, O., et al. (1998) *Informal Carers, Results of an independent study carried out on behalf of the Department of Health as part of the 1995 General Household Survey*, Social Survey Division, Office for National Statistics, London, The Stationery Office.

The Royal Commission on Long Term Care (1999) *With Respect to Old Age: Long Term Care – Rights and Responsibilities*, CM 4192-I, London, The Stationery Office.

Senker, P. (1998) *A note on carer's needs,* Prepared for SPRU, Brighton, December 1998.

Sennett, R. (1998) *The Corrosion of Character: the personal consequences of work in the new capitalism*, New York, Norton.

Shackel, B. (1984) 'The concept of usability', in Bennet, J. et al. (eds.) *Visual Display Terminals. Usability Issues and Health Concerns*, Engelwood.

Silverstone, R. (1994) 'Domesticating the revolution – information and communications technologies and everyday life', in R. Mansell (Ed.) *Management of Information and Communication Technologies*, London, ASLIB, pp. 221-233.

Smith, S., Alexander, A., Hill, S., McGuckin, A. and Walker, C. (1993) 'Housing provision for people with health problems and mobility difficulties', *Housing Research Findings*, No. 86, York, Joseph Rowntree Foundation.

Spackman, A. (1998) 'The market spins towards deadlock', *Financial Times*, Weekend April 18/19.

Tang, P. and Venables, T. (1999) 'The application of smart technologies as part of telecare and telemedicine systems', Paper prepared for *International Conference on Smart Homes and Telematics*, Eindhoven, 22-23 February 1999.

Taylor, R. and Ford, G. (1981) 'Lifestyle and ageing: three traditions in lifestyle research', *Ageing and Society*, Vol. 1, pp. 329-345.

Toffler, A. (1981) *The Third Wave*, New York, Morrow.

Twigg, J. and Atkin, K. (1994) *Carers Perceived: policy and practice in informal care*, Open University Press.

Westra, J. (1994) 'H.O.U.S.I.N.G. – housing older users: selecting ingredients, negotiating gerontechnology', Paper presented at BESTA International Conference, Lillehammer.

Wilkinson, H. and Mulgan, G. (1995) *Freedom's Children. Work, Relationships and Politics for 18-34 Year Olds in Britain Today*, London, Demos.

Wilson, B., Evans, J., Emslie, H. and Malnick, V. (199?) 'Evaluation of NeuroPage: A New Memory Aid', *Journal of Neurology, Neurosurgery and Psychiatry*, Vol. 63, pp. 113-115.

Wooton, R., Loane, M., Mair, F., Allen, A., Doolittle, G., Begley, M., Mclernan, A., Moutray, M. and Harrison, S. (1997) 'A Joint US-UK study of home telenursing', paper presented at *TeleMed 97*, November 27-26, London.

United States General Accounting Office (1997) *Telemedicine Federal Strategy is Needed to Guide Investment*.

United States Office of Technology Assessment (1995) *Health Care Online: The Role of Information Technologies*.

Zuboff, S. (1988) *In the Age of the Smart Machine: the future of work and power*, Heinemann.

Appendix 4

Web Resources

Project participants

Joseph Rowntree Foundation
http://www.jrf.org.uk/jrf.html
Scottish Homes
http://www.scot-homes.gov.uk/
SPRU
http://www.sussex.ac.uk/spru.imichair

Echelon and Lon Works suppliers

Echelon
http://www.echelon.com/
Zytron
http://www.ourworld.compuserve.com/homepages/zytron

EIBus

Siemens
http://www.siemens-industry.co.uk/instabus.casestud.edinvar.htm
EIBA
http://www.eiba.be/
Busch-Jaeger
http://www.suedwestfalen.de/homepage/35006/35006_e.html

Other protocols and *Smart Homes* organisations

COST219
http://www.stakes.fi/cost219/
X-10
http://www.x10.com/homepage.htm
HBS (Japanese)
http://www.hbs.co.jp/

BATIBUS
http://www.invirtuo.com/batibus.index1.htm
CEBUS
http://www.cebus.org/
CEDIA
http://www.cedia.org/cedia
Home Automation Association
http://www.homeautomation.org/
Foundation Smart Homes
http://www.smart-homes.nl/
Proplan
http://www.proplan.co.uk/
Honeywell Controls
http://europe.hbc.honeywell.com/home/homeautomation.htm
INTEGER
http://www.integerproject.co.uk
CDC Central Data Control
http://www.cdc.uk.com/
Control Network Solutions
http://www.control-network-solutions.co.uk/
Intelligent Systems
http://www.intellsys.com/isha.htm
Smart Systems
http://www.smartsystems-inc.com/default.html
Home Automation Times
http://www.homeautomationtimes.com/
Home Systems Magazine
http://www.gohomesystems.com/
Popular Home Automation
http://www.pophome.com/
Bluetooth
http://www.bluetooth.com
FireWire
http://developer.apple.com/hardware/firewire/

APPENDIX 6

GLOSSARY OF TERMS

This glossary is intended as a guide for people who genuinely do not understand some of the terms we have used in our report. More thorough and detailed definitions exist but these should be adequate to explain what we are trying to convey.

Bandwidth
The amount of electronic information that can be passed down a cable. In many ways this is the 'size' of the cable, although the amount of information does not depend necessarily of the physical cross section of the wires but also on the number of wires, how they are arranged and the quality of the wire. Bandwidth does not only apply to metal cables but also to Fibre Optic cables.

Bus System
A dedicated set of wiring specifically installed for the purpose of transmitting data to and from electronic devices within a building.

Co-Axial
A kind of cabling (most commonly found as the aerial wire in the home) where a single core wire is surrounded by a second ring of wire.

Communication Protocols
The agreed 'language' that electronic systems use to pass information to each other. As well as setting out the actual electronic 'words' the systems will use, the protocol will also define how 'loud' and at what 'pitch' the messages will be sent as well as what responses are required to confirm that the information has been received.

Computer Peripherals
A generic term for the devices used by a computer that fall outside of the basic requirements of processor, monitor, keyboard and mouse. These will include printers, scanners, external storage devices, etc.

Heating Ventilation and Air Conditioning (HVAC)
The bundle of mechanical services used to control environmental conditions in the home.

Information and Communication Technologies
The bundle of technologies relating to the electronic storage and retrieval of information and the transmission of such information. Storage and retrieval is typically the function of a computer system, while communication can range from telephony (both land line and mobile) to the internet and more specific computer networks (such as those found in offices).

Infra-red
A wavelength of light beyond the visible spectrum, infra-red can be used as a method of transmitting signals. The most common application in the home would normally be in remote control units.

Iris Recognition
In a similar manner to fingerprints our eyes have a unique and identifiable pattern. Iris recognition systems use cameras to view and analyse the patterns of the iris with a much higher level of certainty than can be applied to say a fingerprint.

Kbits
A unit of data volume; in the cases used in this report it relates to the volume of data that can be transmitted by a specific medium each second.

Microprocessor
A series of complex electronic circuits on a silicon chip. These carry out the calculations for any electronic product, from timers and calculators to large computer systems.

Minitel
A French version of Teletext.

Optical Fibre
The use of glass fibres as a medium for the transmission of information. In a similar way to electrical wiring optical fibres can be used to transmit data, but instead of using electrical current optical fibres use light. This allows huge amounts of data to be transmitted through a relatively narrow cable. Telephone and cable television systems use optical fibres for transmission but

convert this signal to more conventional electrical signals in the home or workplace.

Personal Data Assistants
A small computer with limited functionality, PDAs were developed as a sort of electronic filofax, combining diary, address book, notebook and alarm clock together. More recent PDAs have featured links to personal computers handwriting recognition and e-mail and fax facilities.

Plug and Play
Equipment that is designed to be fully compatible and recognisable by the network and software it will be connected to. Plug and play equipment should be able to be connected to and configured by the system with little to no input from the user.

Powerline
The use of existing electrical cabling for the purpose of transmitting data to and from electronic devices within a building. Powerline transmission sends a data signal at a different frequency to that used for normal electrical current transmission which can then be detected by devices connected to the circuit.

Prestel
A text based service similar to Teletext but containing specific commercially orientated information. Prestel can only be accessed by people or organisations who have subscribed for specific sets of information (such as share prices or travel information).

RDS
Radio Data Signalling, in addition to the music or conversations normally transmitted over the radio there is also some additional data. In its earlier forms RDS was, and still is, used to send signals to electricity meters to let them know when peak and off peak usage should be measured. Currently far more information is sent including the name of the station (which may then be displayed on the radio) and the current time. RDS is also used by radios in cars to identify the best reception for a particular station and to adjust its tuning as appropriate.

Seismic Sensors
Developed from sensors used by geologists, seismic sensors measure vibration. Now used in security alarms they can detect the vibration made by the glass in a window being broken as well as the window being moved.

Smart Cards
Cards similar in size and shape to a credit card but with a microprocessor embedded in them. Smart cards can contain data about the person they belong to that can be read either by inserting them in a machine or remotely over short distances.

Telemedicine
The remote delivery of medical services, primarily in the home, by the use of telecommunication links. Telemedicine can range from remote diagnosis by a doctor from symptoms verbally described to the transmission of detailed x-ray or photographic images by a nurse to a doctor back at the surgery or hospital.

Teletext
Generic term used to describe text-based information services broadcast alongside television signals and readable via suitably equipped televisions. Teletext services generally contain news and entertainment information and are provided by the television broadcaster as a part of their service.

Teleworking
The practice of conducting work activities remotely from the workplace utilising computer and communications systems. Teleworking can range from having the work telephone diverted to, for example, your home to being able to access and alter data stored on mainframes and servers in the main office from a remote location over a conventional telephone line.

Twisted Pair
A kind of cabling where two relatively thin wires are twisted together. The term twisted pair can also be applied to wires with bundles of pairs of wires where the wires will only be used in twos. Telephone cabling in the home typically uses a twisted pair for transmission of sound and data.

User Interface
The method or methods by which the user of an electronic device conveys their intentions to the device and receives feedback. On a computer for example the user types on a keyboard and points and clicks with a mouse and receives feedback from this on the screen of the monitor.

Warden Call Systems
Emergency communication systems fitted in accommodation that is supported by a warden (such as dwellings for the elderly or people with

disabilities). Warden call systems can be used to either send an emergency alarm or to allow a two way communication system direct between warden and the person occupying the dwelling.